Simple Ways to Pray for Healing

Matthew Linn, S.J.
Sheila Fabricant Linn
Dennis Linn

ILLUSTRATIONS BY FRANCISCO MIRANDA

Paulist Press
New York/Mahwah, New Jersey

Acknowledgments

We want to thank the following people for their help in the preparation of this book: Mary Jo Brauner, Walter & Mary Hanss, Barbara & Dr. Morton Kelsey, Maria Maggi, Antonio Martinez Baez, Jr., Jim Reid, Judy Ryan, Rev. John Sachs, S.J., Rev. Robert Sears, S.J., Dr. Douglas & Frances Schoeninger, Sr. Eleanor Sheehan, C.S.J., Donna Stone, Rev. Leo Thomas, O.P., Anna Verstegen, Rev. Flora Wuellner.

Book Design by Saija Autrand, Faces Type & Design.

IMPRIMI POTEST:
D. Edward Mathie, S.J.
Provincial, Wisconsin Province of the Society of Jesus
December 2, 1996

Library of Congress Cataloging-in-Publication Data

Linn, Matthew.
    Simple ways to pray for healing / Matthew Linn, Sheila Fabricant Linn, Dennis Linn.
      p. cm.
    Includes bibliographical references.
    ISBN 0-8091-3762-3
    1. Prayer—Christianity. 2. Spiritual healing. 3. Intercessory prayer. I. Linn, Sheila Fabricant.
II. Linn, Dennis. III. Title.
    BV215.L56 1998
    248.3'2—dc21   97-30789
                                                  CIP

Published by Paulist Press
997 Macarthur Boulevard
Mahwah, N.J. 07430

Printed and bound in the
United States of America

Table of Contents

We dedicate this book to

Marguerite Doyle Banovetz
Jacob & Libe Schreft Fabricant
Fanny & Louis Nasher Kalis
Leonard & Agnes May Doyle Linn

in gratitude for all their
simple and heartfelt prayers for us.

Introduction

Earlier this year we were invited to make television programs for a Hungarian satellite network that broadcasts to three million dispersed Hungarians from Finland to Israel. We recorded the programs before a live audience of 250 people gathered in a church in Budapest. During one of our talks Sheila mentioned baking brownies because Dennis and Matt like to eat them. As the audience listened intently through their headphones to the Hungarian translator, they looked puzzled and then the entire group burst out laughing. We later found out that what the translator had said was the Hungarian equivalent of, "Dennis and Matt like to eat little girl scouts."

Although our Hungarian friends may not have understood the difference between little girl scouts and chocolate pastries, we were happily surprised by how easy it was to communicate with them. Our presentations were based upon the eight simple ways of praying contained in this book. We chose these eight processes as the basis of our retreat in Hungary and as the content of this book because they are the prayer processes we have returned to most often in our ministry. For twenty-five years Dennis and Matt have given retreats and workshops to at least a thousand groups in over forty countries, with Sheila joining our team fifteen years ago. Our participants have come from a wide variety of religious, cultural and educational backgrounds. Their experiences lead us to believe these prayer processes are universally healing.

Perhaps the reason these eight simple ways of praying are so healing is that they integrate contemporary spirituality and psychology with the proven wisdom of the *Spiritual Exercises of St. Ignatius.* (St. Ignatius was the founder of the Jesuits, by whom all three of us were educated.) Also, these ways of praying are simple enough for small children, yet profound enough to touch sophisticated adults.

When Dennis and Matt first began writing about healing prayer in 1974, our readers were primarily charismatic Christians. Since then, our audience has widened considerably and so has interest in prayer for healing. One turning point was the publication of Dr. Larry Dossey's book, *Healing Words,* which was on the *New York Times* bestseller list for many months. Dr. Dossey is a highly respected physician, formerly Chief of Staff at Humana Medical City in Dallas. The National Institutes of Health (NIH) has invited Dr. Dossey to be co-chairperson of a panel that will study the medical effects of prayer. One NIH project collected over 250 empirical studies verifying the healing effects of religious practice that includes prayer. Dr. Dossey concluded that "*not* to employ prayer with my patients was the equivalent of deliberately withholding a potent drug or surgical procedure" and "will one day constitute medical malpractice."

In an article, "Should Physicians Prescribe Prayer for Health?" the prestigious *Journal of the American Medical Association* concluded, like Dr. Dossey, that they should. Interest in healing prayer is now so widespread that *Time* magazine recently devoted its cover story to the evidence that prayer brings healing of body, mind and spirit.

Perhaps this growing interest in prayer is a symptom of an evolutionary shift in consciousness that is taking place all around us. While many Christians fear the twenty-first century will bring a violent end to the world, we wonder if in fact it is an end to an old way of living, and the beginning of a new stage in human development. Most of us have heard that we use only five to ten percent of our brain and we take this to mean that if we studied harder or memorized more facts, then we would use more of our brain. However, some theories of brain function suggest that the real problem is not how hard we try, but rather where we focus our attention. Our focus has been on manipulating the material world around us. Only five to ten percent of the neocortex, the distinctly human part of the brain, is needed for this. It seems possible that the rest of the neocortex has been unused because it is intended for something different: higher consciousness and spirituality (that which transcends space and time). We were made for prayerful contact with God and even our brains develop most completely when we pray.

We write as Christians who have experienced the healing love of Jesus in our own prayer lives. However, we hope this book will be used by people of all faiths. Experiments on prayer indicate that its efficacy is not determined by the private religious affiliation of the one who prays. Dr. Larry Dossey says,

As long as love, empathy and compassion are present, the prayer seems to work.
. . . I feel there is a great lesson in tolerance in these experiments in prayer.
When it comes to prayer, no religion has a monopoly.

We are writing for anyone who wants to give and receive the healing love of God as he or she understands God.

This is a book about simple ways to pray for healing and it is meant to be prayed rather than only read. Healing is a process and thus you may wish to take as much time as you need to pray through each chapter before you move on to the next one.

For those who wish to share this book with others, see the section "Process for Group Sharing." For those who wish to explore these prayer processes more deeply, several of them are the subjects of entire books, described in the section "Resources for Further Growth by the Authors."

CHAPTER 1

Healing Through Gratitude

For over twenty years, we have begun every retreat in the same way. We share our moments of gratitude from the previous year, and ask participants to do the same. If I (Sheila) were to do this now, I would recall two related moments. The first is that about a year ago Denny and I began the process of adopting a child, after a few years of trying to conceive. The type of adoption we are pursuing is one in which we can take a lot of initiative in finding a child. After we were approved by a local adoption agency, we wrote to several hundred friends, many of whom are involved in ministry or health care, asking them to watch and pray with us for a child. Since then, we are constantly receiving letters and phone calls expressing support and offering help—not to mention a car seat, baby clothes, diapers, toys, etc., etc. Denny and I agree with the African proverb, "It takes a village to raise a child," and we both feel immense gratitude for the way our "village" has gathered around us.

The second and related moment began seven years ago in Mexico, just before we were married. Knowing that we like handmade things, our Mexican friends took us shopping for dishes as a wedding gift. In the artisan market in the small town of Valle de Bravo, we found simple clay bowls. They came in two sizes: larger ones for soup or salad and smaller ones for dessert. We brought a dozen of each back to the U.S. Our dinner guests often admired these bowls, and we wanted more to give as gifts.

We give a retreat in Mexico every January, and for the next few years after we were married, wherever we went we looked for bowls. But we could not find any exactly like ours. Finally, this year we returned to Valle de Bravo. We headed straight for the market where we had bought our bowls six years earlier.

We found the small ones, and bought two dozen of those. But there were no large bowls. I asked a local man where the bowls were made. He directed us to a place a few blocks away. As we went, we held out the car window a small bowl that we had just bought and asked passersby, "Where do they make these bowls?" One person said, "No one around here makes those bowls any more." Another directed us to a place a few more blocks away. Yet another sent us back where we started. . . .

After an hour of this, a man pointed and said,

"Across the street."

"Are you sure? There's nothing there—just old shacks."

"That's where they make the bowls. Go over there."

We walked across the street, into a shack with a dirt floor. There was no furniture, and a very old man was sitting in the corner on a pile of stuff covered with a cloth. I showed him my small sample bowl and asked, "Do you have any of these bowls?" He looked carefully at the small bowl in my hand and said, "No." Then I noticed that the stuff under the cloth where he sat was the color of clay. I said, "Can I look at what you're sitting on?" He stood up and lifted the cloth. There were dozens of large bowls, exactly the kind we wanted. He didn't have any *small* bowls, but he had 105 large ones. . . . We bought them all. They cost only twenty cents each, but we felt as if we had found a lost treasure. As far as we knew, this was the only place in all of Mexico that still made exactly the kind of bowls that belong in our home.

One day in February, after we had returned home, I was reflecting on the bowls and how glad I was that we didn't give up looking for them or settle for something other than the ones we really wanted. Then it occurred to me, "The bowls are about our child. We found the right bowls after we watched and waited for a while, and we'll find the right child, too."

In March we were offered a child who was due to be born in July. We began preparing our home. Six weeks later, the birth mother changed her mind and decided to keep that child. As Denny and I grieve, I keep returning in my prayer to the memory of the bowls. I recall the moment when the old man pulled away the cloth, and we knew we had found just what we needed. I breathe in again my gratitude and let it fill me. I need to keep going back to that moment of gratitude, to give me hope and strength as we wait for a child.[*]

---

[*] Our son, John Matthew, was born ten months after this was written.

Positive memories of moments for which we are grateful remind us that God has cared for us in the past and will care for us in the future. Perhaps that's why St. Ignatius of Loyola, whose *Spiritual Exercises* have guided retreatants for centuries, emphasized that when we are stuck in desolation, memories of consolation (or gratitude) can often return us to a sense of wholeness and freedom.

GRATITUDE HEALS OUR RELATIONSHIPS, OUR BODIES AND OUR WORLD

Such memories also remind us that we have cared for others in the past, and we can continue to care for them in the future. For example, our friends Joe and Eileen were having serious marital problems. They tried all sorts of communication techniques, without success. One day Eileen returned from a medical checkup with a diagnosis of cancer. Crying as she told Joe the news, she said, "You have given me so much love. Promise me that if I die, you will remarry and give that same love to another woman." Then she shared with Joe all the ways he had loved her for which she was grateful—her positive memories

of their marriage. Joe responded by sharing the things he was grateful for about Eileen. These memories of how they had loved each other in the past restored the bond between them. They knew they could love each other again for as long as they still had left to be together. When Eileen returned for more medical tests, her cancer was gone.

Eileen's experience is an example of how positive memories of gratitude can heal not only our relationships, but our physical health as well because they cause physiological changes in the body. (For example, pessimistic men between the ages of forty-two and sixty are twice as likely to die from heart attacks as are optimistic men.)

Returning to memories of gratitude has the power to strengthen our bodies, heal broken relationships and give us hope at times of loss. Going back to positive memories can also affect entire groups and social structures. For example, Rabbi Harold Schulweis wondered how he and other Jews could tell their children about the Holocaust without destroying their capacity to believe in human goodness. Then he began hearing about "rescuers," people who risked their lives to save Jews during World War II. After studying them for decades, Rabbi Schulweis now believes there were at least half a million rescuers and that we must hold on to their memory:

> The most important commandment of the post-Holocaust era should be the recognition of goodness. Because this alone can struggle against the curse that says, "We had no friends, we have no friends, we will never have friends." That paralyzes our leadership. It kills the future. If all you have is a hammer, then the whole world is full of nails.
>
> . . . Let the church celebrate its truest heroes and the synagogue publicize their spirit. Jews need Christian heroes, Christians need Jewish heroes. For that heroism from the other side helps break down the vicious polarization.

Partly as a result of Rabbi Schulweis' work, there is now a growing cooperation between Jews and Christians who are committed to preserving the memory of rescuers.

I have experienced the healing effects of this myself. Many of my father's Jewish relatives in Poland were killed by the Nazis. Although this happened before I was born, I have always been acutely sensitive to stories of the Holocaust. For example, although I have travelled all over the world, I was afraid to visit countries

where concentration camps were located. Then I began reading stories of rescuers. It seemed that I could not get enough of them; I wanted to know about every act of kindness during the Holocaust. Gradually, I felt more able to face the evil that also happened, to the point that this year we visited Auschwitz. We prayed there for healing between Jews and Germans.

I needed to know about goodness before I could fully face evil. Positive memories empower us with the strength and courage to face and heal the hurts we have experienced as individuals and as groups.

GRATITUDE AND BELONGING

Another example of how going back to positive memories has affected an entire group or social structure is that of Alcoholics Anonymous. The co-founder of Alcoholics Anonymous and the author of the 12 Steps was Bill W. He understood the importance of going back to positive memories for which we are grateful, to give us what he would call a sense of belonging. When Bill was twenty-two years old, a socially awkward and insecure person, he attended a party. He took his first drink, and then another. Writing about this experience, he said,

> I felt that I belonged where I was, belonged to life; I belonged to the universe; I was a part of things at last. Oh, the magic of those first three or four drinks! I became the life of the party . . .

Bill's first drink gave him what he most needed at the time to survive: a sense of belonging. Seventeen years later, Bill was still drinking. His doctor told Bill that he would probably go crazy and die of alcoholism. One night, alone in his hospital room, Bill cried out in desperation, "If there be a God, let him show himself to me now!" Then,

> Suddenly my room blazed with an indescribable white light. I was seized with an ecstasy beyond description. . . . For the first time I felt that I really belonged. I knew that I was loved and could love in return.

After this experience, Bill W. never took another drink.

The accounts of Bill's first drink and his hospital room conversion are very similar. He even uses the same words to describe both experiences: "I felt that I belonged." We believe that all addictions and compulsions, in their beginning, were the best way we knew at the time to belong to ourselves, others, God and the universe. As a self-conscious young man, Bill's alcoholism was the best way he knew at the time to belong. He recovered only when his hospital room conversion experience gave him a better way to belong.

Bill W. went on to write the 12 Steps, which have guided millions of people to recovery from alcoholism and other addictions. We believe Bill began the 12-Step movement to give others the same sense of belonging that healed him. Thus, in writing the 12 Steps, Bill reflected on his positive memories of whatever had helped him stay in touch with that sense of belonging he felt in his hospital room. Each of the 12 Steps summarizes moments that helped him on his own journey of recovery. The same process that Bill W. used in writing the 12 Steps is used at each 12-Step meeting. Participants are invited to share their moments of belonging (their everyday stories of recovery) so that everyone present can draw strength and healing.

Bill W. called the sense of belonging "one of the greatest rewards of meditation and prayer," since once we have it, "all will be well with us, here and hereafter." The following prayer process is intended to help us find our own memories of gratitude that can give us a sense of belonging.

❦ *Prayer Process*

We begin each prayer process by paying attention to our breathing. Breathing can be a way of getting in touch with gratitude as it reminds us of our connection to all of creation. Because air currents cause such a complete mixing of the earth's atmosphere, each time we inhale we take in at least one atom of air breathed by every person on earth within the last few weeks. Since the elements of air circulate through the entire chain of life, breathing is literally a way of connecting ourselves to all of creation. Each time we inhale we can gratefully take in all creation. Each time we exhale we can gratefully bless all creation.

1. Close your eyes and breathe deeply, breathing in the love of God that surrounds you.

2. Recall a moment from the past for which
you are grateful,
— a moment in which you experienced
belonging to yourself, others, God
and the universe
— a moment in which you were able to
give and receive love. Perhaps you will
think of the day you were married,
the birth of your child, a conversation
with a friend, an experience with
nature, a special moment in prayer, a
time when you stood up for what you
believed.

3. Whatever moment comes to you, imagine yourself back in that situation once
more and relive it. See the people who
were with you, hear their voices or other
sounds, recall what you smelled and what
you felt with your skin.

4. Breathe in deeply, letting the love and
gratitude you experienced in that moment fill you once more.

CHAPTER 2

Healing Through Affirming Love

The previous chapter explored the first movement of prayer: recalling moments for which we are grateful, especially moments when we have been loved. This chapter focuses on letting those moments grow inside us until we can enter into a flow of giving and receiving affirming love.

It is only in the light of affirming love that we know who we are. I (Sheila) first learned this from Dr. Conrad Baars, author of *Born Only Once*. Dr. Baars wrote that all of us have been born once—physically. But many of us have not yet been born psychologically because no one has yet sufficiently affirmed us. We have been born *only* once and we are still waiting for our second, psychic birth: our birth as our true self.

For example, last week, Dennis and I attended our weekly exercise class. All the other students were absent. The teacher, Jamie, focused her attention on the two of us and repeatedly told us, in a warm and loving voice, how well we were doing. I have always seen myself as having zero athletic ability. Yet I left that class feeling more physically confident than I can ever recall, because of Jamie's affirming love.

The movement of affirming love has four parts. First, if we want to give affirming love, we recall moments when we have known our own lovableness and goodness. Jamie, for example, is at home in her body. Her confidence in her own athletic ability allowed her to see athletic ability in me. The second part of the movement of affirming love is noticing goodness around us. Dennis and I were the only students in Jamie's class last week and she focused her attention upon us. Third, we let that goodness move us with delight. And fourth, we reveal our delight in some way. Jamie did this with appreciative smiles and words of praise. All I had to do to participate in this flow of affirming love was stay in Jamie's presence and open my heart to take in her affirmation of me.

AFFIRMATION AND SEEING

Jamie was giving me a gift that is as essential for human development as food and as basic to the nature of the universe as the atom. Jamie *saw* me with eyes of love. We know who we are as human beings only when we are seen by another who loves us. The loving gaze of a parent toward his or her child literally creates the child's sense of self. The impact of one who sees begins even at the subatomic level. For example, one of the most startling discoveries of modern physics is the Heisenberg Uncertainty Principle. It says that we cannot predict with certainty the direction and the velocity of a subatomic particle, because the observer affects what he or she is observing. Moreover, many physicists now believe that the very nature of matter is changed by being observed: subatomic particles apparently change from waves to particles when they are seen by a human being.

Similarly, if we consider the circumstances of a person's early life, we cannot predict with certainty how his or her life will evolve because the effect of those who see (or fail to see) this person will make such a difference. Studies of resilience in children from deeply troubled backgrounds have found that a critical factor in their ability to succeed is the presence of even one loving adult who can bond with that child. Bonding is *seeing* and being seen. Alice Miller calls the one who sees the "enlightened witness." The enlightened witness is a person who stands unreservedly on the side of the child, sees that child's reality through eyes of love, and validates it.

Perhaps an intuition for the enlightened witness, the Heisenberg Principle, and the way an observer causes waves to manifest themselves as particles is why the Judaeo-Christian tradition holds that God is personal. Of course God is infinitely more than what we know of persons, but it seems to us that God is *at least* personal—because only One who is personal can see us. Thus, healing prayer begins with allowing ourselves to be seen through infinitely loving eyes, thereby affirmed, and born as our true selves.

WE PASS ON THE GIFT OF AFFIRMING LOVE

When we are affirmed, especially at critical or vulnerable moments in our lives, or by people with whom we have a significant bond, that affirmation is imprinted upon us. We carry with us a gift that we will never lose and that we will pass on to others. For example, when Ann was a poor college student she mistakenly wrote five bad checks. The bank fee for overdrafts was $10 each and Ann could not afford to pay $50. She went to the bank and asked to see the Vice President. Ann apologized for the overdrafts and explained her financial situation. Seeing Ann's goodness, the Vice President said, "Anyone can make a mistake," and cancelled the $50 in fees. Today, when Ann's children blunder, her instinctive response is to see their goodness and say lovingly, "Anyone can make a mistake."

Another example of how we pass on affirming love is recent research on the role of a "doula" in labor support. The doula is not a mid-wife or part of the medical team. She is a woman caregiver whose only task is to accompany another woman during the process of labor and delivery. The doula never leaves the mother's side and never criticizes. She is constantly affirming, nurturing and encouraging. Several different studies demonstrate the medical benefits of having a doula present. For example, first-time labor is an average of two hours shorter, the chance of cesarean section is reduced by fifty percent, mothers need less pain medication and have fewer complications, etc.

But even more impressive to us is the effect upon maternal behaviors. Those mothers who have a doula present show significantly more maternal behaviors toward their new baby. This continues as the child grows, with the mother likely treating her child in the same loving way that she herself was treated by the doula. A woman is uniquely vulnerable and open during labor and delivery. If she is intensely affirmed by a mother figure at this time, the experience imprints powerfully upon her and can overcome years of negative messages from her own mother. She will then instinctively and automatically pass on to her child the affirming love she has received.

My own mother was limited in her ability to love unconditionally. As I prepare for a child, I've wondered, "How can I, as an adoptive mother, replicate the experience of having a doula with me?" I have found myself instinctively gathering my most loving women friends around me, making an extra effort to stay in touch with them and take in their love for me. I cannot affirm myself. What I can do is put myself in situations where I am likely to receive affirming love, consciously take it in, and let it grow within me.

AFFIRMING LOVE AND LEARNING

Affirming love is so essential that we cannot learn or do anything well without it. For example, recent studies of memory suggest that it is not really in the brain. Rather, memory is in a field that surrounds us and our brains are like TV receivers that tune in to that field. Related to this, Harvard researcher Dr. Howard Gardner proposes that there are distinct intelligences for various areas of learning, e.g., linguistic intelligence, mathematical intelligence, musical intelligence, etc. It seems that all these intelligences are contained in the field of memory that surrounds us, and learning involves tuning in to that aspect of the field. But we cannot do this fully unless we are in a loving relationship with a living model of that intelligence. For example, if I want to learn music—not just musical scores and techniques, but the living heart of music—I need another human being who loves me and who loves music. This person makes a bridge between me and the intelligence of music, and empowers me to develop my own capacity to tune in to that intelligence. Thus, human beings do not learn most deeply from televisions or computers, but rather from other human beings with whom they are in a flow of affirming love.

HEALING THROUGH AFFIRMING LOVE
AT HOME AND AT WORK

The opposite of affirming love is denial. Many of us have received so much denial that we are now literally "wired" for it. Harville Hendrix, a noted marriage therapist, teaches his clients a process called "flooding." In this process, one spouse verbally affirms the other in increasingly loud and more intense ways to the point of screaming at the top of his or her lungs such things as, "You're so wonderful I can't stand it! I love you so much!" Dr. Hendrix believes this intensity of positive energy and emotion is necessary to counteract the intensity of negative energy attached to all the critical comments and other forms of denial that most of us have received. Our brains literally need to be rewired in a positive direction, and marriage is an opportunity for this to happen. In his thirty years of studying happy marriages, Dr. John Gottman has found that in these marriages, the number of positive comments expressing gratitude for one another during conflict resolution is at least five times more than negative comments. In marriages that will end in divorce, spouses make fewer positive comments than negative ones.

There are simple, everyday ways in which we can give and receive affirming love. For example, a social worker at a large health care facility has a way of easing tensions at work. He encourages employees to gently touch their supervisors on the outer forearm during conversations or in passing by. Most people are not threatened by being touched in that area, and this small gesture of warmth generates a flow of love in the workplace.

Another man has begun a family custom that he calls the Annual Letter. All year he writes down loving thoughts and saves objects and photos that commemorate special moments in his daughter's life that year. On her birthday, he collects them into an Annual Letter that is sealed in a big envelope and presented to his daughter. Together they take the Annual Letter to the bank and place it in the safety deposit box on top of all those from previous years. On her twenty-first birthday, she will be able to open all the letters, a collection of twenty-one years of her father's love for her.

GIVING AND RECEIVING AFFIRMING LOVE
THROUGH CREATED THINGS

For people who grew up in homes lacking in affirmation, the way into a flow of giving and receiving affirming love often begins with nature or even inanimate objects. We can begin with anything—a stone, a leaf, a blade of grass, a favorite dish or tool. All of creation is intended to be a source of affirmation and nourishment. When it fails to do that for us, we suffer as surely as when we are being denied by human beings. The German poet Rilke wrote,

> For our grandparents, a house, a well, a familiar tower, their very dress, their cloaks, were infinitely more intimate: almost everything a vessel in which they found and stored humanity. Now there come crowding over from America empty, indifferent things, pseudo-things, dummy things. The animated, experienced things that share our lives are coming to an end and cannot be replaced. We are perhaps the last to have still known such things. On us rests the responsibility of preserving, not merely their memory (that would be little and unreliable), but their human . . . worth.

We often hear that the illnesses of modern life are materialism and consumerism. The idea is that we care too much for material things and have more of them than we need. I believe our problem is exactly the opposite. I believe we care too little for material things and have less of them—less of their essence—than we need. Most of the things that surround us were made without affirming love. They do not nourish us, nor do they evoke our love or wonder. For example, today the average five-year-old child has owned 260 toys, few if any of lasting value. Fifty years ago, the average five-year-old child had five toys, likely made with care from natural materials. Perhaps we want more things because we are starved for matter that can nourish us, just as people who consistently overeat junk food may actually be starving for nutrients.

I experienced this once when we were invited to a dinner at an exclusive restaurant. Most of the other guests arrived in elegant clothes, the women (and men) glittering with jewelry. There was enough food for a group four times our size, including huge roasts and expensive seafoods. I felt overwhelmed by all the glitter and excess, and increasingly isolated. Dessert was served from a buffet table

full of elaborate pastries. At the end was a bowl of fruit. I put three strawberries on my plate, returned to my seat and began to eat them very, very slowly. It seemed to me somehow important that I be entirely present to those strawberries and truly enjoy them. As I did, I gradually felt less isolated and was able to reach out to the other guests.

I am not sure if it was I who was appreciating the strawberries or the strawberries who were appreciating me. All I know is that stopping to be present to one thing enabled me to reenter a flow of giving and receiving affirming love with other people. Affirming presence to matter helps us develop a habit of affirming presence to people because it's a form of contemplation. Contemplation opens us to the goodness of God within us and all around us.

JESUS NEEDED AFFIRMING LOVE, TOO

Our emphasis upon the importance of affirming love cannot be reduced to the psychological need for self-esteem. Rather we believe it is foundational to the spiritual life. We cannot follow Jesus or live like him until we know that we are loved. Jesus himself could not live as the Messiah until he knew that he was loved. At his baptism Jesus heard the words, "This is my beloved son in whom I am well pleased" (Mk 1:11). Only then could he begin his ministry. Later he needed to hear those same affirming words again (Mk 9:8). All of us, even Jesus, need to take in affirming love and let it grow within us before we can move on in prayer or in life. We need to know what Nelson Mandela quoted when he was inaugurated President of South Africa:

> Our deepest fear is not that we are inadequate. Our deepest fear is that we are powerful beyond measure. It is our light, not our darkness that most frightens us. We ask ourselves: Who am I to be brilliant, gorgeous, talented and fabulous?
>
> Actually . . . who are you *not* to be? You are a child of God. Your playing small doesn't serve the world. There is nothing enlightened about shrinking so that other people won't feel insecure around you.
>
> We were born to make manifest the glory of God that is within us. It's not just in some of us, it's in everyone, and as we let our own light shine, we consciously give other people permission to do the same. As we are liberated from our own fear, our presence automatically liberates others.

❦ *Prayer Process*
(We suggest this process if you are alone.)

1. Close your eyes and breathe deeply, breathing in the love of God that surrounds you.

2. Recall a moment when you felt loved—a moment of belonging to yourself, others, God or the universe. Go back in your imagination to that moment and reenter the scene. Breathe in that moment, letting it remind you of your lovableness and your goodness.

3. Open your eyes and notice the things or people around you. See if one particular person or one particular thing appeals to you and draws your attention. Whoever or whatever it is, allow yourself to notice its goodness and its beauty.

4. Let yourself be moved by that goodness and beauty, allowing your heart to respond with appreciation and delight.

5. Reveal your delight in some way, especially nonverbally, e.g., by letting your eyes grow soft, smiling, extending your hands, touching, etc.

❦ *Companion Prayer Process*

(We suggest this process be done in groups of two or three.)

1. Close your eyes and breathe deeply, breathing in the love of God that surrounds you.

2. Recall a moment when you felt loved and experienced your own goodness.

3. Open your eyes and become aware of your companion(s). Notice his or her goodness. Ask yourself what you like about this person or how this person is a face of God.

4. Let your heart be moved by the goodness of the other.

5. Take turns sharing with one another how you see each other's goodness.

CHAPTER 3

Healing Our Image of God

We have found that prayer and healing are possible only to the extent that we have a positive, loving image of God. Few of us will open ourselves or become vulnerable to a God of whom we are terrified. Yet many of us carry deep fear of God, because we have been taught to see God as punitive. The ultimate image of this is a judgmental God who keeps a list of our mistakes and may vengefully throw us into hell if the list gets long enough. Moreover, we become like the God we adore. If our God has the same unloving attitudes we are trying to heal in ourselves, we are not likely to get very far.

I (Dennis) experienced in my own life how my judgmental image of God blocked my prayer for healing. Even worse, the more I prayed to this God the more judgmental I myself became. In our book *Good Goats: Healing Our Image of God,* I shared the story of what helped me. There I recounted that, like some of my German ancestors (although I don't wish to stereotype Germans), I was a judgmental, self-righteous person. For years I prayed for healing of my self-righteousness and nothing worked. And then one day I noticed that my self-righteousness had disappeared.

After years of trying, why had I changed so suddenly? I changed because my image of God changed. My God had been a self-righteous German. My God (I had an all-male God at the time) would sit on his judgment throne and, like a good self-righteous German, see all the mistakes in everyone else. If he didn't particularly like what he saw, he could distance himself from others and even send them to hell. And if my God could do that, then no matter how hard I prayed, I tended to act the same way. Now I realize that we not only repeat the characteristics of our ancestors and parents whom we "adore," but we also repeat the characteristics of the God that we adore. My self-righteousness disappeared when my image of God changed from a "German God" who vengefully threw people into hell, to one who loves me at least as much as Sheila or Matt or others who love me the most. In order to continue healing my image of God, I needed to rethink what I was taught about hell.

Joining Jesus in Hell

I did this a few years ago when Sheila and I celebrated Holy Week in Jerusalem. On Holy Thursday we joined thousands of other pilgrims at the site where tradition claims Jesus celebrated his last supper. On Good Friday the same crowd of people pushed and shoved their way with us up the Via Dolorosa where the events of Jesus' crucifixion occurred. But, on Holy Saturday, when we went to the place Jesus called "hell" in order to celebrate with him his descent into hell (1 Pet 3:19), we found only one other person there.

Hell, "Gehenna" in Greek, comes from the Hebrew "Gehinnom" which means "Valley of Hinnom." This valley is located in the southeast corner of Jerusalem. Jeremiah cursed this valley because an ancient cult had performed human sacrifice there. For centuries thereafter, including in Jesus' time, this unholy and unclean site served as the Jews' garbage dump. As long as any Jew could remember, deteriorating garbage had fueled Gehenna's continuous fire. Perhaps one reason Jesus used Gehenna or hell as an image of what happens to us when we behave in an unloving way was to remind us of what psychosomatic medicine has recently discovered. If we act in unloving ways, not only will we feel like garbage, but we will also find our physical body and our whole self deteriorating just as did Gehenna's garbage.

The only other person in hell that Holy Saturday was a shepherd caring for his herd of goats. Trying not to disturb him, we sat down at the far side of hell and began our Holy Saturday vigil. A short while later, another man dressed as a shepherd entered the valley and greeted us. He walked through hell for about a quarter of a mile. Then he suddenly turned around and walked quickly back to us.

He told us he had spotted some Arab children whom he was afraid would come and stone us. (Because of the recent massacre of Palestinians by an Israeli

in Hebron, some Arabs were hostile toward us Americans whom they perceived as supporting Israel.) He insisted on walking us to the other end of the valley where we would be safe. For twenty minutes this shepherd with his staff guided us safely through hell, making sure that no one harmed us. We thanked him and sat down, now at the most extreme edge of hell, to resume our Holy Saturday vigil.

About an hour later, as we turned to leave we noticed him sitting high up on the wall of Jerusalem's old city that overlooked the valley. He had posted himself there as our sentry, still guarding us to be sure that nothing would happen to us in hell. When we had finally exited hell, we waved to our shepherd who then climbed down from his sentry post and disappeared into the old city.

THE DESCENT INTO HELL

My experience parallels what I have recently learned about the meaning of what Holy Saturday celebrates, Jesus' descent into hell. Catholic theology contains various traditions and explanations for the descent into hell. For example, I was taught that Jesus descended into hell in order to free the just souls who were awaiting their redemption.

However, in the footnote for 1 Peter 3:19 the New Jerusalem Bible offers a second tradition. In this tradition Jesus descended into hell to preach, teach and

heal the hard-hearted and unrepentant. Thus Jesus goes to heal even "the chained demons mentioned in the book of Enoch" or the unrepentant in Noah's time who were punished by the flood because they "refused to believe." If we define hell as the adamant choice to close one's heart to God, then it would seem that hell is the one place where God cannot be. But theologian Hans Urs von Balthasar explains that by going there anyway, Jesus chooses to "enter into solidarity with those damning themselves." Thus, although from our side it seems that we can choose to reject God, from Jesus' side he refuses to abandon us and will not leave us to our own worst selves. As von Balthasar says, "Even what we call 'hell' is . . . always still a christological place."

I learned about this second tradition at about the same time that I was doing an internship at a treatment center for addicts. In treatment, one comes face to face with one's own hell. We have all probably had experiences of hell. Hell is alienation, the inability to give and receive love. Probably all of us at one time or another, like those at the treatment center, have been caught up in a compulsive pattern or an addictive behavior that alienates us from those who love us.

During my internship at the treatment center, I met many loving families and friends who refused to honor the destructive choices of a drug addict or an alcoholic. Rather, they chose to enter into the addict's hell in order to intervene. The late Dr. Robert Stuckey, whose treatment centers have treated over 20,000 patients, claimed that inter-ventions can be made on the most unrepentant and hard-hearted addicts, those who have no intention of changing. Recovering addicts often share their stories of how their loving family and friends entered into their hell. Even though these addicts were powerless over their addiction and had no intention of ever repenting or changing, their loved ones remained with them until they could take their first steps toward healing.

In a similar way, Jesus' descent into hell is his refusal to accept our choice of destruction as final. Holy Saturday proclaims that Jesus' mission is to demon-strate solidarity with us by even, if necessary, descending into our hell and being with us there until his healing presence renews us enough to take the first steps in rising with him on Easter. We cannot know with certainty the final outcome of those who seem to choose hell. However, most major Catholic theologians agree with Karl Rahner, perhaps the greatest Roman Catholic theologian of the twentieth century, that we can hold out the "unshakable hope" that all will be saved.*

That Holy Saturday when I visited hell in Jerusalem, I felt this unshakable hope because everything was just as it should be. The goats, the symbol of those meriting the eternal punishment of hell (Matthew 25), were there. But so was Jesus. That day in hell we experienced the Good Shepherd who not only vigi-lantly watched over the goats but also protected us in our journey through hell and would not leave us until we had emerged safely.

The goats and the Good Shepherd set the stage for what I most wanted to do in hell. I had looked forward to spending Holy Saturday in Jerusalem so that I could give thanks for all the people in my life who have not left me to my destructive choices or to my worst self. Like Jesus, these people chose to enter into my hell and stay with me there until their healing presence could renew me. As I gave thanks for each person, God became for me less a self-righteous German and more a God who loves me at least as much as those who have loved me the most.

---

* You may be having many questions, such as "What about free will?" "What about passages like Matthew 25 that seem to say that God does send people to hell?" etc. For a complete dis-cussion of such questions, see our book *Good Goats: Healing Our Image of God* (Mahwah, NJ: Paulist Press, 1994). Although the position we have taken here and in *Good Goats* may be dif-ferent from what many Christians were taught, we want to assure our readers that it is well within the parameters of Roman Catholic orthodoxy.

WHAT ABOUT HITLER?

Perhaps you are thinking, "But Dennis, you're a basically good person. You have never done anything really evil. What about someone like Hitler?" Consider the following prayer, composed by a Jewish woman who died at the Ravensbruck concentration camp. It was written on wrapping paper and found next to a dead child:

> Lord, remember not only the men and women of good will but also those of ill will. But do not only remember the suffering they have inflicted on us; remember the fruits we have brought thanks to this suffering—our comradeship, our loyalty, our humility, the courage, the generosity, the greatness of heart which has grown out of all this, and when they come to judgment, let all the fruits we have borne be their forgiveness.

If a Jewish woman can pray this for the worst of my German relatives, is not God at least as loving as she? If we recall those who love us the most, we will discover a God who is at least as loving as the best of us.

❦ *Prayer Process*
(We suggest this process if you are alone.)

1. Close your eyes and breathe deeply, breathing in the love of God that surrounds you.

2. See the faces of the one or two people who have loved you the most. Breathe in the special gift of each person, such as gentleness, loyalty, listening, wisdom, etc.

3. Take a moment to be with God as you understand God and appreciate how God loves you in these same ways.

4. If there is any way you can't experience God as loving you at least as much as the person who loves you the most, be with your hurt and longing. Breathe in God's love and let God love you just as you are.

❦ *Companion Prayer Process*
(We suggest this process be done in groups of two or three.)

1. Close your eyes and breathe deeply, breathing in the love of God that surrounds you.

2. Recall a moment when you felt especially close to God and able to trust God. Perhaps it was a moment of healing, a time when you felt deeply loved by another human being, the birth of your child, etc. Return to that moment in your imagination and breathe in once again your sense of being held safely in God's care.

3. Now recall a moment when you felt distant from God, a time when it was more difficult to trust. Perhaps there was an accident or other tragedy and you could not understand why God would allow it to happen; perhaps you did something you felt ashamed of and you didn't know that God loved you just the same; perhaps you were alone and it was hard to feel God's love when you were missing human love. Or, perhaps you are most in touch with an area of your present life where you find it hard to trust God, e.g., your finances, your health, your marriage, concern for one of your children, an addiction in which you feel stuck, etc.

4. Form groups of two or three. Let the person on the right in a group of two (or in the middle of a group of three) take the role of God. If you are in the role of God, imagine that you have a frightened and lonely child before you who doesn't trust you. As God, how would you reach out to your child? Perhaps you would take his or her hand or reach out your arms and embrace your child. Do whatever God within you wants to do.

5. The person on the left (or the two on the outside of a group of three) breathe in love from your companion, knowing that God loves you at least this much. Breathe it in especially into that moment when you found or now find it hard to trust God. Continue giving and receiving the love of God in silence for a few minutes.

6. Reverse roles so that the person on the left (or on the outside) reaches out as God and the person on the right (or in the middle) receives God's love.

CHAPTER 4

Healing Through the Five Stages of Forgiveness

The previous three chapters have presented the foundation for praying for healing. This chapter introduces a process for healing a hurt through prayer. Once we gratefully recall how we have been loved (Chapter 1), take in that love and let it deepen (Chapter 2) and have a loving image of God (Chapter 3), we can let that love touch our hurts.

Imagine yourself walking down a dark alley. A tall shadowy figure jumps from behind a garage, knocks you down on the pavement and runs off with your money. What is your first thought? Is it "I forgive you"?

If you couldn't immediately say, "I forgive you," you are very normal. You are also probably in touch with the natural process that eventually leads to forgiveness and healing of emotional wounds. To heal physical wounds we have a natural process of bleeding to cleanse the wound, then platelets release fibrinogin to start the clotting, and finally a scab forms which will fall off on its own. If we rush the process and pick off the scab, we have to start all over. Similarly, in her work with the dying Dr. Elisabeth Kübler-Ross discovered that we move through a natural process of grieving in accepting the hurt and loss of death. This process has five stages: denial, anger, bargaining, depression and acceptance of death.

We discovered that, because there is a loss in any hurt, the process of healing hurts involves the same five stages of grieving. Since hurts with their losses

are healed to the extent that we forgive, these are also the five stages of forgiveness. The stages are: 1) denial (I'm not hurt); 2) anger (it's their fault); 3) bargaining (I will forgive them if. . . .); 4) depression (it's my fault); and 5) acceptance (I can accept and forgive what happened because I experience gifts coming out of the hurt). Dying people will go back and forth between the stages and some may go through them in a different order. But dying people will eventually reach acceptance if they have a significant person who will love them with whatever they are feeling. So, too, we will naturally move through the five stages of forgiveness if we take in love from God and others with whatever we are feeling.

DENIAL

I (Matt) was about to experience the five stages as I drove home from visiting my parents through a peaceful snowfall on Minnehaha Creek Parkway. Suddenly another pair of headlights met mine and dove at me. I tried to swerve off the road but it was too late. Metal was smashing all around me. My little red Geo Metro plunged toward the giant elms. I spun the wheel, narrowly missed one tree and plowed into a snow bank. The other driver didn't stop and moments later I heard a loud crash as he hit a truck head on.

Miraculously I stepped out of my car shaking but without a scratch. My shattered Metro would take two months of body shop repairs. I walked over to the hit and run driver. He was drunk and he wanted to fight. I swallowed my anger and walked away to safety. In shock, I denied the extent of my hurt and anger and told myself how lucky I was to be alive. I was still shaking as I drove the crippled car home, but denial kept me from being overwhelmed.

ANGER

In the morning daylight I looked at my car and saw the crumpled driver's door. I realized a drunk driver had nearly taken my life. That afternoon I drove back to my parents' house. I took a different route because I was afraid to drive on Minnehaha Creek Parkway. Although I was on through streets most of the way,

I felt afraid every time I approached an intersection. I didn't trust that other cars would stop, and I kept slowing down to avoid being hit. I was suddenly afraid of more than other cars. During the next few weeks, I locked doors that I wouldn't have locked before, and then I went back again and again to be sure I had locked them. Nothing felt safe.

Gradually I realized how much of my normal confidence I had lost, and I began to feel angry. The police told me the accident wasn't my fault. Sam, the other driver, had tested drunk. His record included seven arrests, three DWI's, and three warrants out for his arrest. Why was he released seven times to traumatize people like me even when he had no insurance? I was glad that this time he was in jail and would pay for his crimes. My angry pleasure at the thought of Sam behind bars helped me feel safer and less vulnerable.

At whatever stage I am, it helps simply to experience my feelings and to let myself be loved by God and others. At this stage, I angrily shared the car wreck story with my friends and God and let them love me with my anger. In prayer I kept hearing Jesus tell me that he, too, was angry at the damage caused by drunk drivers. I recalled Jesus' anger when he threw the moneychangers out of the temple, and I imagined him helping me throw drunk drivers out of bars and into jail. Gradually, as I felt loved in my anger, my fantasies of getting even with Sam diminished.

BARGAINING

As I became less angry my prayer gradually changed from, "Punish Sam and keep him in jail forever so he'll never hurt another person," to "Help Sam mend his ways." I realized that being thrown out of bars and into jail hadn't helped Sam. He needed A.A. I was now in the bargaining stage where I wanted Sam to change. Bargains are conditions we want others to meet before we'll forgive them. Bargains reflect our needs, and I needed my sense of safety restored. My bargain was, "I will forgive you if you get help for your alcoholism and stop endangering other people's lives." Since Sam was so self-destructive, there was little chance of sobriety unless someone reached out to him. Then it dawned on me that maybe the best way I could protect myself was by becoming his friend and leading him to A.A.

DEPRESSION

Everything in me said, "Find someone else." Since the accident I felt so vulnerable and shaky that I didn't think I could convince a duck to swim. "He needs an expert, not me," I thought. I was now in the depression stage, feeling my own inadequacies. The things I didn't like in myself were the same things I didn't like in Sam. I didn't like his lack of concern for others and that he felt so inadequate to change and get sober. Yet I wanted to be unconcerned about Sam. And I was having a hard time changing my own feelings of inadequacy. As I shared my feelings of inadequacy with Jesus and let him love me, I gradually felt more confident and willing to at least visit Sam in jail.

When I called the jail, I learned that Sam had been released and was driving again. I was relieved that I could go on with my life and have nothing more to do with him. Then I realized that I still felt afraid of him every time I drove a car. I needed to stop avoiding Sam at every intersection and face him in some way. I decided to call Sam and ask if he would like to go out to dinner to celebrate the fact that we were both alive after a terrible accident. Maybe we could even get around to talking about A.A. It did seem that God was guiding me to reach him, because his last name had two pages in the phone book and no "Sam." I picked a number and it was busy. I tried another number and Sam answered.

As I talked with Sam, I was surprised I could feel so much compassion for him, and even more surprised when he said to call back Saturday so we could arrange a pizza celebration. He wasn't in on Saturday. I tried three more times to arrange a meeting, and each time he avoided committing himself to a specific time. I finally realized he really didn't want to meet me nor get me angry by directly refusing my invitation. As I sensed his fear of me and his efforts to avoid me, he no longer seemed like a big monster whom I had to avoid lest I be crushed in my little car.

Now I felt equal to Sam. Just by trying to meet with him I had overcome my fear. The next time I visited my parents I realized afterwards that I had taken my old route along Minnehaha Creek Parkway, and I had not felt compelled to slow down at every intersection. I had recovered the sense of safety that Sam took from me. I was now willing to forgive him even if he never changed.

He didn't change and six months later the insurance company called to ask if I would testify against him in court because he refused to pay for damages. At first, I was back in the depression stage (it is normal to cycle back and forth between the five stages). I thought, "I can't help him. He'll never change." But as I let myself be loved in my depression, I gave myself credit for having reached out to help him once. I knew I could do it again by requiring him to take responsiblity for his actions. I was willing to try, even if Sam still didn't change. As it turned out, he started paying rather than face the court.

ACCEPTANCE

I was now in touch with a gift to reach out to a person who had hurt me, even if he never changed. When I begin to experience gifts coming out of a hurt, I enter the acceptance stage. I was not grateful for the accident. But I was grateful for how I had grown from it, for the new ways I could give and receive life with God, others and the universe. After surviving an accident that could have

been fatal, every time I drive down Minnehaha Creek Parkway I am reminded that each day is a gift. Now at the beginning of each year I ask, "What do I want to do before I die?" rather than putting things off for another ten years that I may never have. That question led me to take a wonderful week to go fishing with my father before he died two years later. In the acceptance stage we are more grateful for new life and we go fishing!

❦ *Prayer Process*
(We suggest this process if you are alone.)

1. Close your eyes and breathe deeply, breathing in the love of God that surrounds you.

2. In your imagination go back to the scene of a hurt and let yourself reexperience it.

3. Share with Jesus or with God as you understand God whatever feelings you are most in touch with, and what you most need at this time.

4. Let God love you with those feelings. Watch what Jesus says and does for you and breathe it in.

❦ *Companion Prayer Process*
(We suggest this process be done in groups of two or three.)

1. Close your eyes and breathe deeply, breathing in the love of God that surrounds you.

2. In your imagination go back to the scene of a hurt and let yourself reexperience it.

3. Share your feelings with Jesus or with God as you understand God.

4. As you get in touch with how you have been hurt, what do you most need? Perhaps it is the strength to accept what you can't change, such as the death of a loved one. Perhaps it is the courage to change a situation that needs to be changed. Share this, too, with Jesus or with God as you understand God.

5. Now open your eyes and read Mark 3:1–6, the story of Jesus healing the man with the withered hand.

6. Then take the hand of your companion to form groups of two or three. As your companion takes your hand, recall how Jesus reached out to the man with the withered hand and restored him to life.

Let the person on the right in a group of two (or in the center of a group of three) be Jesus, holding the withered hand(s) and pouring life into it. If you are Jesus, feel his fearless compassion that restores life even on the sabbath when it was forbidden to heal. With each breath let Jesus' compassionate love flow from your heart through your hand and into the hand of the person for whom you are praying.

If you are on the left in a group of two or on the outside of a group of three, continue being yourself in whatever memory you felt hurt and withered. Recall what you need to be restored. Breathe this in through the hand of Jesus that is holding your withered hand. Continue in silence for the next few minutes while Mark 3:1–6 is being read.

7. Now silently reverse roles. If you gave Jesus' love, now receive it into your withered hand. If you received it, now become Jesus and give his healing love. Continue praying in silence for the next few minutes.

CHAPTER 5

Healing Relationships with the Deceased

The previous chapters were about taking in love from those who love us the most and forgiving those who have hurt us. But what if the person who loves us the most or the person we most need to forgive is dead? This chapter is about how we can give and receive love and forgiveness through prayer with those who have died.

During a retreat several years ago, we found out just how healing this can be. We prayed with eleven people for various problems, including depression, chronic back pain, sexual addiction and alcoholism. We asked each one, "When did your problem begin?" One person said, "Three years ago," another said, "Eight years ago," etc. Then we asked, "Did anything significant happen then?" In seven cases a close friend or family member had died. As these seven people began in prayer to grieve and to give and receive love and forgiveness with those who had died, their problems diminished or disappeared. It seemed that their present problems were only symptoms of a greater hurt in the past: a death that cut short the flow of love and forgiveness. Their experience is consistent with numerous studies of the effects of unresolved grief on physical and emotional health. For example, after the death of a loved one we are fourteen times more likely to have a heart attack and fifteen times more likely to suffer clinical depression.

THE SOUL LIVES WHERE IT LOVES

How is it possible to give and receive love with people who have died? We believe the soul lives where it loves, and we suspect most families have experi-

enced this. For example, only once in her life has my (Dennis') mother awakened because of a shooting pain in her right leg. She knew her father had been having a similar pain, and she began praying the rosary for him. Almost immediately she received a phone call saying that her father had just died. She believes the pain was her father's way of coming to her and gently leading her to pray for his final journey.

Last year Sheila and I received a call telling us that my father had had a heart attack and was in intensive care in the hospital. As we boarded a plane to go home, I sensed my father's presence all around us. It seemed dense and yet full of light. I told Sheila that I thought he had just died. Forty-five minutes later when we landed to change planes, we called and found out that he had indeed died.

Love is the connective tissue that makes all things one, and since love is eternal, love can connect us with the deceased forever. As St. Paul told us,

> Love does not come to an end . . . In short, there are three things that last: faith, hope and love; and the greatest of these is love (1 Cor 13:8–13).

Following is a reflection from the Eastern Orthodox Church on how the deceased live where they love:

> But God is the heaven of faithful souls.
> Heaven therefore is in us
> in so far as God is there.
> May we not conclude that our soul
> is a sanctuary of the holy souls
> as it is a temple of God?
>
> Are we not justified in thinking that we bear them
> (after a fashion) in ourselves
> and that they are incomparably closer to our soul
> than the little babe
> of which she is the tabernacle
> is close to its mother's heart?
>
> (From "The Splendor of the Liturgy,"
> by Maurice Zundel)

I experienced this closeness to a deceased person with my cousin, Mary Jane. During her life, I always liked to be around her. Regardless of how stressful a day I had had, whenever I was in her presence I always experienced a deep stillness and peace. When Mary Jane died, her stillness and peace moved inside me and have been there ever since. Mary Jane has made her home within me and is "incomparably closer" to me than even the pregnant mother is to the babe who makes its home in her womb.

WE CONNECT WITH THE DECEASED OUTSIDE SPACE AND TIME

Although we can affirm with the Eastern Orthodox that the deceased make their home within us, they are not limited to specific points in space or time. Because they live in God, they are omnipresent and eternal. But science has discovered that so are we. Our mind cannot be limited to specific points in space (our brain) or in time (the present moment). Rather studies such as those at Princeton affirm that our mind transcends space and time:

> For about a decade, studies done at Princeton University's Engineering Anomalies Research Laboratory have indicated that subjects can influence the outcome of random physical events and can mentally convey complex information to other subjects from whom they are widely separated, even by global distances. These studies show not only that a sender can mentally transmit detailed information to a receiver on the other side of the earth, but also that the receiver usually "gets" the information up to three days before it is sent.

What gives our minds the capacity to live outside of space and time, such as receiving information from across the globe three days before it is sent? Love, empathy, and compassion, which are the basis of prayer, are also what researchers find facilitate our mind's capacity to move into a realm outside of space and time. This is the realm of universal and unconditional love.

Perhaps that is why so many people who have had near-death experiences (NDE's), in which they are met by an unconditionally loving and compassionate Being of Light, have so readily experienced themselves as outside of space and time. While such a person's physical body is lying on an operating table, he or she

may observe family members interacting outside in the hallway or even miles away at home. Not only does the Being of Light typically help such people to reexperience and learn from each event of their past, but they are also sometimes given "personal flashforwards" in the form of glimpses of their own future. When they return from a NDE, they are more likely than other people to be able to anticipate future events or to sense events in the present that are occurring at a distance.

THE DECEASED WANT TO HELP US

During the NDE, it is common to meet loved ones who have already died. The person having the NDE realizes that these loved ones have been present all along, sending love and care. Such awareness of the loving presence of deceased people caring for us happens not only during NDE's, but in everyday life. For example, Jim experienced this in his relationship with his mother who had died twenty-six years earlier. Her inability to communicate emotional warmth had hurt Jim deeply as a child. Over fifty years later, he still struggled with the effects of her coldness and emotional denial upon his life. His anger at her was so great that he could not visit his mother's grave or even look at her picture without feelings of revulsion. Although Jim loved his wife dearly, his anger at his mother spilled over into his marriage and Jim would inadvertently speak to his wife in blaming and critical ways. A deeply prayerful person, Jim feared he was not really acceptable to God and scrupulously tried to be "good."

One day in prayer Jim felt very still and especially receptive to God's love. Once more he asked Jesus to help him forgive his mother. He had an image of himself at age seven, crying silently. Then he saw his mother, also as a child of seven crying silently. Jim realized his mother's childhood suffering was similar to his own, and he felt great compassion for her.

Then he had a third image, of his mother as an adult woman about his own age. He heard her say, "I know what a mess this has created for you and I'm so sorry." This was the first time in Jim's experience that his mother had ever expressed feelings or asked forgiveness. Her love was utterly real to Jim, more real than what he normally experiences as reality.

Jim told us that this was the most significant healing of his entire life. His feelings of resentment and anger toward his mother totally disappeared. He now experiences a warm flow of loving energy whenever he thinks of her. As he says, "Before, it was as if I had no mother. I got my mother back." During the year since this experience, Jim's blaming and critical behaviors toward his wife have gradually ceased. His relationship with God has relaxed into an easy confidence that he is loved just as he is and that "God is really *for* me." He is a gifted psychotherapist, and he now has a matter-of-fact certainty that God will help his own clients, especially with unresolved relationships with their deceased loved ones.

Although Jim's mother had been dead for twenty-six years, she was able to help Jim in a real and powerful way, giving him the love he desperately needed from her and did not receive as a child. Jim experienced the meaning of 1 Corinthians 12 and of the Doctrine of the Communion of Saints: we are all one body in Christ. For Jim this came through vivid images and distinct words. For others it may come simply through a felt sense of the deceased person's care. Regardless of how it happens, we can be assured that God and the deceased always want to give and receive the most love possible with us. Love never ends and it is never too late to give and receive love and forgiveness.*

❦ *Prayer Process: Lazarus Prayer*

1. Recall, or read, the story of Jesus raising Lazarus from the dead (Jn 11:32–44). Close your eyes and breathe deeply, breathing in the love of God that surrounds you. Continue breathing deeply and with each breath fill yourself with Jesus' compassion for the deceased.

---

* For a more extensive discussion of the theological and scriptural basis for praying for the deceased from a Christian perspective, see our book, *Healing the Greatest Hurt* (Mahwah, NJ: Paulist Press, 1985). This book includes studies of the effects of unresolved grief on health, as well as healing ~~prayer processes for those who have hurt us,~~ those we miss the most, past generations, suicides, and babies (miscarried, aborted or stillborn).

2. With your right hand make a fist. Let that fist become as hard and as immovable as the stone that covered Lazarus' tomb. Who is the deceased person behind that stone for whom Jesus is inviting you to pray?

3. Before asking Jesus to help you move the stone, share with him how you feel about this person's death. Like Martha and Mary who complained to Jesus, "If you had been here, my brother would not have died," you may wish to express your disappointment. On the other hand, perhaps you feel relief. After having expressed all your feelings, listen to what Jesus most wants to say back to you.

4. When you feel ready, push back the stone with Jesus and imagine that the deceased person is, like Lazarus, bound from head to foot. Unbind the person, beginning with the forehead. When you have uncovered the eyes, look into those eyes and share what you most want to say.

5. When you have said everything, continue unbinding the person until you get to the heart. As you unbind the heart, look inside it and see what it is that the person most wants to say to you.

6. Continue to say and do with that person whatever will most fill both of you with life. Perhaps you wish to take him or her to a favorite spot, or introduce new members of your family, or have this person fill in some hurt place in your life (as Jim's mother did for him). If you are praying for a miscarried, aborted or stillborn baby, perhaps you wish to name the child and baptize it with Jesus.

7. If it seems right, make a space for this person in your heart. Perhaps imagine putting a rocking chair or a candle there, and invite him or her and Jesus to make their home in your heart. As they do so, feel the warmth of their light filling your heart. Take deep breaths, breathing in all that they want to give you.

CHAPTER 6

Shoe Prayer:
Healing Through Intercession

During our years of giving retreats, we've noticed how often people want prayer not for themselves but for someone else. Frequently they want prayer for a person they feel very close to, whose pain they carry. Other times they want prayer for a person who is hurting them and they want God to change that person. Since our retreatants usually want prayer for people who are not present, we teach them how to intercede for others at a distance.

We first learned the power of intercessory prayer while we were giving a retreat in Dallas. Although many of the participants were divorced, seven were so estranged that they didn't even know where their former spouse lived. These seven people spent the retreat asking God to heal both them and their estranged spouses. When we returned a year later, five of the seven shared that within two months after the previous year's retreat, their spouses contacted them. These people had not heard from their spouses for five to fifteen years. Although they had no idea where their former spouses lived, we believe their intercessory prayers reached across space and time and brought healing.

We are not alone in our belief. Science, too, is beginning to recognize the healing power of intercession. Based on a discovery known as Bell's Theorem and on subsequent experiments, physicists have discovered that,

> If two subatomic particles that have been in contact are separated, a change in one is correlated with a change in the other, instantly and to the same degree . . . even if they are separated to the opposite ends of the universe.

Likewise, when two human beings are connected, prayer from one "creates a simultaneous change" in the other. Cardiologist Randolph Byrd studied this at San Francisco General Hospital. He randomly divided 393 cardiac patients into a control group and another group that would receive intercessory prayer over ten months. Although neither the staff nor the patients knew who was receiving prayer, the prayer recipients had significantly fewer complications. They were five times less likely to require antibiotics. None went into cardiac arrest, compared to twelve in the control group. Similarly, none needed a mechanical ventilator, compared to twelve in the control group. None of the prayer recipients died, compared to three in the control group. In almost all of the twenty-six medical categories that were tested, patients fared better when they received prayer. After examining this study, even Dr. William Nolan, who has written a book expressing his skepticism about faith healing, said, "Maybe we doctors ought to be writing on our order sheets, 'Pray three times a day.'"

PRAYING FOR PEOPLE WHO HAVE HURT US

Perhaps the group of people most difficult to pray for are those who have hurt us. We have found one prayer process so healing that we use it on nearly every retreat. This process is based on the Sioux prayer, "Great Spirit, grant that I may never criticize my neighbor until I have walked a mile in his moccasin." We call it the "Shoe Prayer" because it involves trading our right shoe with another person. (We've done this in over forty countries and it always worked well until we got to Japan. Unbeknownst to us, all two hundred retreatants had already taken off their shoes and left them at the church door. . . .) Wearing another's shoe as we pray is a symbolic way of helping us compassionately enter the world of the person who hurt us.

One person who did this prayer with us was Gereon. In 1944 Adolph Hitler's soldiers killed Gereon's family. Gereon was so eager to take revenge that he became involved in three different plots to kill Hitler. Thirty-five years later, Gereon still had not been able to forgive Hitler. Then, at a Shoe Mass during one of our retreats, Gereon traded his right shoe with his neighbor and was astonished to receive a military boot just like Adolph Hitler's. We led participants in prayer, encouraging them to walk in the shoe of the person they were praying for and to try and become like that person.

As Gereon tried to walk in Hitler's shoe, he felt the tightness of that military boot. He tried to enter more deeply into Hitler, sitting like a soldier with his back as stiff as a rod and his feet stubbornly dug into the ground. As he became aware of the terrible constriction and rigidity of Hitler's world, he felt compassion. He was able to forgive Hitler for everything except Hitler's hardness of heart. But this hard heart felt strangely familiar. Suddenly Gereon broke into tears as he realized that Hitler's hard heart felt just like his own hardened heart that for thirty-five years had been unable to forgive.

Gereon continued to pray, now walking in his own left shoe and allowing God to love him with his own hardness of heart. Gereon thus avoided the temptation of codependents, who tend to walk in other people's shoes before they have first walked in their own. We can give to another only what we have received. Thus it is important to stay in our own shoe and take in the love we need.

When we have taken in enough love, we will naturally feel moved to walk in the other's shoe and give to him or her what we have received. By the end of the Mass, Gereon had walked in his own shoe long enough and taken in enough of God's healing love for his own hardness of heart that he could offer it even to Hitler. Later, as he bent down to remove the military boot and return it to his neighbor, Gereon realized that for the first time in thirty-five years he could bend over without the ever present sharp pain in his back. Gereon had literally taken Hitler off his back.

When we intercede by praying the Shoe Prayer as Gereon did for Hitler, we intercede in the same way that Jesus does. When Jesus intercedes, he becomes like us in everything but sin (Heb 2:14–18; 4:15; 7:25). In becoming like us in everything but sin Jesus is always choosing to walk in our shoes.

INTERCEDING FOR PEOPLE WE LOVE

We can pray the Shoe Prayer not only for those who have hurt us, but for any person at a distance whose world we want to compassionately enter. For example, this past year Mary Jo called and said, "I've just been diagnosed with breast cancer. I'm scheduled for surgery in two weeks." Her voice was full of fear, especially that the cancer would spread to her lymph system. Mary Jo told me (Sheila) that the abnormal cells were at the ten o'clock position on her right breast. As I prayed for her each day, I tried to walk in her shoe by putting my hand on the same place on my own body. I asked God the Mother (the motherly aspect of God, as in Isaiah 49:15) to let my right breast be a channel of Her vital, nurturing feminine life and to send that healthy energy into Mary Jo's right breast.* I imagined her breast being filled with gentle, healing light. It seemed that Mary Jo, God the Mother and I became one in a flow of healing life, a flow that could wash away any illness.

The next time I talked with Mary Jo, she told me how cared for she felt by God the Mother. She was full of peace by the time of her surgery. The follow-up tests found no cancer in her lymph system. Mary Jo now experiences a deeper connection to her feminine identity than ever before. She wants to devote her life to women's issues (especially breast cancer) and to caring for other women as God the Mother cared for her.

My ability to send health to Mary Jo's body through imagery is not surprising,

---

* There is no history of cancer in my own family and I am not afraid that I will ever develop it. Thus, this part of my body feels full of extra life and I was not likely to overidentify with Mary Jo's illness. If I were afraid of breast cancer, I think I would have needed to "walk in my own shoe" first and receive healing for my fear before praying for Mary Jo. Otherwise I might have communicated fear rather than peace and healing to her.

since scientific studies suggest that one person's imagery can change the physiology of another person. For years the medical community has accepted biofeedback, in which we voluntarily control our own blood pressure, peripheral skin temperature, brain waves, etc. through the use of imagery. Now, carefully designed studies by Dr. William Braud find that our imagery can also affect the physiology of *another* person *at a distance* "in degrees that are only slightly less robust than when that person tries to make those changes in his or her own body." It seems to us that the power of prayer builds upon and amplifies this natural human capacity.

Another example of this happened before our retreat in Mexico. When we went water skiing with Tomas, our local host, he fell and tore the ligaments in his leg. Tomas could neither straighten his leg nor stand on it. He went to see the best specialist in sports medicine, who worked with many of Mexico's professional athletes. This doctor said that he had seen the same injury at least a hundred times. It would take a month of bed rest before the injured leg would heal.

The next afternoon I (Matt) was teaching a group the Shoe Prayer. I decided to pray for Tomas. I tried to enter his world, by standing on only one foot. I breathed in Jesus' power to heal and let Jesus' strength flow into my leg.

Later that afternoon we returned to Tomas' home, where we were staying. Tomas opened the door! He told us that he had been lying in bed and suddenly felt a warmth in his torn leg. He wasn't a person who believed in healing prayer, but his leg felt so different that he gradually tried to straighten it. To his surprise his leg moved normally without a trace of pain. This had happened at the exact time that I was praying for him by trying to walk in his shoe. Tomas doesn't like to waste money. He said, "The next time, before I rent crutches I'm going to first get someone to pray for me." Then he offered to open an office for us across the street from the crutch rental store.

❦ *Shoe Prayer Process*

The following prayer invites us to enter the world of another person. Some people are already too deeply enmeshed in the world of another, whether it's a person they are very close to or someone who has hurt them deeply. For such people, who are already carrying another's reality at the expense of their own, this prayer can be a way of carrying the other in a different, more aware and liberating way. The first steps of the prayer are especially important, in which we get centered in ourselves by "walking in our own shoe."

1. Find another person's right shoe and put it on your right foot, keeping your own shoe on your left foot. Close your eyes and breathe deeply, breathing in the love of God that surrounds you.

2. Get in touch with a person you feel drawn to intercede for. Perhaps it is someone who hurt you as in the case of Gereon, or a person in need, such as Mary Jo or Tomas. Let the right shoe represent the world of that person.

3. First focus your attention on your own left shoe, as a sign of walking in your own world. Now notice how you feel when you think about the person for whom you want to pray, especially how you feel in your body. Perhaps you feel a lump of sadness in your throat, a knot of anger in your stomach or anxious tension in your neck. Place your hand on that part of your body, gently caring for it. Spend as much time as you wish breathing in from God whatever you need before you will be ready to pray for another. Perhaps you want to imagine a trusted person joining you in doing this prayer, especially a person by whom you feel

deeply known, such as a favorite grandparent. During the steps that follow, if at any time you feel overwhelmed by the other person's reality, return to this step.

4. When you feel ready to join Jesus or God as you understand God in offering life to the other person, focus your attention on your right shoe. Ask God to help you walk in the other's shoe and become like that person. Let your body become like that person's body and try to enter into what he or she thinks and feels. Allow your awareness of that person's world to mold your forehead, face, jaws, shoulders, back, hands and feet. What parts are tight with anger, shaking in fear, bent in shame, heavy with sadness or perhaps numb with denial? Do this until you sense your entire body resembles that person's body.

5. When you are in touch with how that person needs healing, ask yourself how the Holy Spirit might be praying within that person. Perhaps the Spirit's prayer is only a few words such as "Be with me" or "Peace." Join the Spirit in praying this prayer.

6. As that person, breathe in the warm light of God's healing love, letting it fill you with all you need. Breathe out any darkness or burden. Continue this in whatever way you wish until you find yourself filled with new life.

7. Now return to being yourself. As you do, you may wish to open your hands and release the other person into God's hands.

8. Healthy intercession leaves *us* feeling full of new life as well as the person we are praying for. If you find yourself still feeling the other person's burdens, return to Step 3 above and take in what you need for yourself.

CHAPTER 7

Praying with Another for Healing

All the ways of praying in the previous chapters can be done alone. However, in our families and communities, we often find ourselves with another person who needs prayer. Yet many of us have little confidence in our ability to pray with another person.

For example, I (Matt) thought the only people who prayed for healing were crazy faith healers on television, saints, or priests who, when giving last rites, were primarily praying for a happy death. At the time, I didn't have the prerequisites of being either crazy, holy or yet ordained. Then I spent a summer living with Mary, a Sioux grandmother who taught me Lakota. After I moved out, she had a severe heart attack. Her family asked me to go to the hospital and pray with her. When I arrived, the nurse told me that Mary's vital signs were failing fast after two weeks in a coma. I took Mary's hand and said,

Mary, this is Matt. I'm here because I love you. Your grandchildren who love you so much told me you were sick. We want to help but we can't do much for you. Jesus loves you even more than we do and he can do whatever you need. So let my hand become the hand of Jesus and let him take you wherever he wants to walk with you.

For another minute I prayed quietly for Jesus to take her home and then left to visit other patients.

On my return past the nursing station, the nurse told me Mary was now out of her coma and asking for me. Mary, who saw I was in a state of shock at her recovery, smiled and said:

> I've been hearing things but I couldn't talk or move. When you took my hand and asked that Jesus take my hand too, he did. We walked across a beautiful field filled with flowers and singing birds. Then Jesus stopped and asked, "Mary, what can I do for you?" I told Jesus you made me so lonesome for my grandchildren that I wanted to go back to them. So Jesus turned around, led me back here and I woke up.

I could hardly believe that with my feeble prayer for her happy death, Jesus had brought Mary back to life. Maybe Jesus was able to do so much because he had already placed so much of his deep love for Mary in my heart that he and I could pray for her with one heart.

I (Sheila) learned to pray with another for healing through my friend, Alex. I had never thought of myself as having a gift for physical healing and I felt inadequate when Alex asked me to pray for his chronic migraine headaches. As I put my hands on his head, I recalled the loving presence of God that I had always sensed in the created world. Since early childhood, I had frequently experienced leaves, flowers, blades of grass, etc. as luminous with the presence of God. It seemed to me that this luminous, loving presence must also fill the cells of our bodies and so I imagined this presence flowing through the veins, arteries, muscles and nerves of Alex's head. To my astonishment, Alex's migraine headaches were often relieved when I prayed for him. He told me once, "I think the reason my migraines go away when you pray is because you love every cell for its own sake."

I (Dennis) overcame my resistance to praying with another person after a thirty-day retreat that I gave to Carol. Because of genetic neural damage in her ears, she had to lip-read what I said. I thought, "Maybe if I pray with Carol, God will restore her hearing." But I didn't have much confidence in my prayers for healing because a friend whom I had recently prayed for had died of cancer. So, I was discouraged and thought, "If someone else prayed with her, or if she went to a special place, she might be healed." I never risked praying with Carol. Thus she left the retreat as deaf as when she came.

A year later I received a letter from Carol telling me, "I can hear dripping water, people behind me, birds, wind . . . it's all like music." Some of her friends

had prayed with her for healing. Even though she still had genetic neural damage, doctors confirmed that her hearing had been totally restored. The doctors
were astounded and so was I. I felt both happy and sad. I was happy that she could
hear and sad that I had not reached out to pray with her. Carol's healing gave
me courage and soon we were ending every retreat by having people pray in twos
with each other for whatever healing they wanted. Although these prayers lasted
only five minutes and were done in absolute silence, we began hearing many stories like Carol's.

For example, Joaquin, a reticent Guatemalan villager who looked as old and
craggy as the mountains where he lived, proclaimed matter-of-factly to seven
thousand people,

> For years I could not hear. When you asked us to pray in twos, my wife
> placed her hands on my ears and began praying. I heard a bell. Then something
> like a door blew open in each ear. Now I can hear everything clearly.

After retreatants like Joaquin and his wife have prayed for five minutes with each other, we always ask questions of the group to find out what happened. Usually one hundred percent of the people report that they feel more joy and peace, and also that they feel closer to the person who prayed with them. That in itself is no small feat, given that depression and alienation seem to be more prevalent today than the common cold. Of those who need some kind of physical healing, about three-fourths report some verifiable physical improvement—or even complete healing, as in the cases of Joaquin and Carol.

HEALING COMES DOWN TO LOVING

What Carol discovered with her friends, or what Joaquin and his wife experienced together, is that healing comes down to loving. For example, when Jesus went to heal Jairus' daughter, he brought with him his friends Peter, James and John, and also the girl's parents (Lk 8:49–56). Perhaps he chose these people because they were the ones who especially loved either him or the little girl.

Sometimes when a sick person asks us for prayer we, too, choose those who can love that person the most. We usually ask three people to lead the prayer: the sick person's best friend, a person who is suffering from the same sickness, and a person who has been healed of that sickness. We choose these people because they have a natural compassion for the one who is sick. As these three people allow the love of Jesus to move through them, often they, too, are healed. We find that healing occurs more often where there is more love because Jesus, the source of all healing, is love.

Contemporary medicine understands the healing power of love. Dr. Bernie Siegel says,

> I am convinced that unconditional love is the most powerful known stimulant of the immune system. If I told patients to raise their blood levels of immune globulins or killer T cells, no one would know how. But if I can teach them to love themselves and others fully, the same changes happen automatically. The truth is: love heals.

Even plants respond to the presence of love and will grow better in the presence of people who appreciate them and even talk lovingly to them. Every cell in our bodies and everything else in creation was spun out of the love of God and responds to love.

PRAYING MORE THAN ONCE

Why doesn't God always heal everyone totally and immediately? We don't know. Sometimes the answer to healing prayer is a risen body in the next life. Often, however, it seems that healing prayer needs to be continued in this life in order to build up more healing love. For example, sometimes the first few times we pray a person will experience peace, the next few times pain might be diminished and finally mobility might be restored. It is as if each time we pray we add more love, allowing more healing to happen.

Our friend Bob experienced this when he prayed with Joan, a blind woman with inoperable cataracts. As Bob and Ed, Joan's husband, prayed with her, she began to see but then her vision got worse again. Bob said,

> Go home and pray together for five minutes each night. Share with each other how you want prayer. Then take turns laying your hands on each other and praying with all the love that Jesus places in your heart. Come back in a month and tell me what happened.

They returned a month later and Joan could see clearly enough to read. She said, "We were going to get a divorce because we felt we had grown so far apart. But praying for each other for five minutes each night showed us how much we really love each other and healed not only my eyes but also our marriage." Sometimes when healing doesn't happen immediately, we are being invited to pray again in order to build up the healing power of love.

GIVING AND RECEIVING JESUS' LOVE

Praying with another is simple. Although the examples we have given involve physical healing, we can pray in the same way for emotional healing. If we are the one giving the prayer, all we do is let ourselves become Jesus. Becoming Jesus means we consciously identify with the loving Spirit of Jesus that dwells within all of us. In this sense we can say that it is "no longer I who live but Jesus who lives in me" (Gal 2:20). So, for instance, when we reach out to pray, we can try to reach out with the same compassion as Jesus, even asking him where he would place his hand, and how he would place it. Then it is just a matter of letting Jesus' love flow from our hearts, through our hands, and into the other person. The prayer can be done in silence, without words, simply filling the person with Jesus' healing love.

If we are receiving prayer, all we need to do is breathe—breathe in the love of Jesus that is coming to us through the hands of the person praying with us. We can imagine breathing that love into whatever part of our body needs it most. (For example, if we have back pain, we can breathe love into our back. If we are praying for healing of depression or for healing of a relationship, we might breathe love into our heart.) We don't have to think great thoughts or have great faith. Rather, whether we are giving the prayer or receiving it, what heals is Jesus' love, a love that was freely given.

❦ *Process of Praying with Another for Healing*
(We suggest this process be done in groups of two.)

1. Share with each other how you want healing (e.g., "I feel depressed," or "I have a backache").

2. Decide who will give the prayer first and who will receive the prayer first. If you are the one to pray first, take some deep breaths and fill yourself with the healing love of Jesus or God as you understand God. As your heart fills with Jesus' love and compassion, place your hand on the other person as Jesus would, with the same care and gentleness and in the same place. In absolute silence, fill that person with the love of Jesus that is flowing out from your heart.

3. If you are the one receiving prayer, all you need to do is continue breathing. Breathe in the love of Jesus that is flowing through the heart and hands of the person who is praying with you. Breathe it into the part of your body that most needs it.

4. After five minutes reverse roles.

(If you are alone, you can still pray for another. Just imagine yourself as Jesus lovingly placing your hand on the person for whom you want to pray. Imagine filling that person with the love of Jesus that is flowing out from your heart.)

CHAPTER 8

The Examen

We want to end this book with the process we use to end each day. Every night we gather together, light a candle, look back over the day and ask ourselves two questions: For what today am I most grateful? For what today am I least grateful? We can ask these two questions in different ways, for example,

When today did I give and receive the most love?
When today did I give and receive the least love?

What moment today gave me the most life?
What moment today drained life out of me?

When today did I have the most sense of belonging to myself, others, God
    and the universe?
When today did I have the least sense of belonging?

After a few minutes of quietly reflecting on these questions, we take a few more minutes to share with one another our experience of the day. In traditional spirituality, this process is called "The Examen." What we are getting in touch with is consolation and desolation. For centuries prayerful people have recognized that it is through these two interior movements that we can discern the guidance of the Spirit within us.

For example, I (Sheila) did the examen one evening after a long trip that involved several plane flights. The day had included many interesting and happy moments, including a warm welcome from our hosts in the city where we arrived.

Yet, when I asked myself what gave me the most life that day, I recalled the few seconds when I played with a child in one of the airports where we changed planes. During the next year, I noticed how often this pattern repeated itself: that no matter how many exciting events were part of a day, children were the source of that day's consolation for me. In general, God's will for us is to do more, whenever possible, of whatever gives us consolation. This is because God, who is a God of life, wants us to give and receive the most life possible. Thus, the examen has helped Dennis and me decide to have children of our own. Noticing that a child in the airport was the source of a single day's consolation might not seem very important. However, such moments can become very important and give direction to our lives as day by day the examen reveals the pattern of what most gives us life.

LISTENING TO DESOLATION AS WELL AS CONSOLATION

Moments of desolation are equally important. For example, as we (Dennis and Sheila) began preparing for a child, we realized that we needed to add another room to our home. Our budget is limited and so we drew the plans ourselves. During our nightly examens, the work we had done on the plans that day was often our consolation as our dreams took concrete form. Then we discovered that our property line is seven feet closer to our house than we had thought. We changed our plans entirely and designed a tall, narrow addition that included a basement and a storage attic. We wanted stairs from one level to another, but the engineer told us we would not have room for stairs. Although it would be inconvenient, we would have to use the existing stairway in the main part of the house. By this time we were experiencing both consolation and desolation over the whole project at our nightly examens.

The evening before the builder was to dig the hole for the foundation, Sheila was away overnight. At 10:30 P.M. the owner of the concrete company called, after three weeks of not returning Dennis' phone calls. He told Dennis that because of our change in plans, he would have to charge us four times more for the foundation than his earlier estimate. The next morning, the builder arrived with his digging machine. Our house is high up from the street, and he had hired a crane for $240 to lift the machine onto our land. Sheila arrived home thirty min-

utes before the crane was due, and Dennis told her the news about the cost of the foundation.

By now, our consolation about the addition had changed almost entirely to desolation. Yet, we had invested so much time already and so had others who were helping us. How could we stop at this point? Then Sheila recalled a friend who was married to the wrong man for thirty years. This friend was full of desolation during her engagement, but she thought it was too late to call off the wedding because the invitations were already out. We said to one another, "It's not too late. We can still stop this." By then the crane was in the driveway. We ran down the hill of our front yard, waving our arms and yelling, "Stop! Stop!" We asked the crane operator to wait and invited our builder up into the house to talk.

As we discussed the whole situation with him, we realized that the expense and difficulty of our plan were no longer worth what we would get out of it. Our builder assured us that he could find other work, and we cancelled the project. We still had to pay the crane operator $240 for his time. But it seemed to us well worth what we had learned: it is never too late to listen to our desolation and say, "No."

We also learned the importance of listening to the interior movements of consolation and desolation at the beginning, middle and end of any decision. Sometimes we feel consolation at the beginning and we act on it without continuing to listen as our plans unfold. As it turned out, our original consolation was leading us to build an addition, but our desolation was warning us that our plans had become too elaborate. We waited two months and a whole new plan emerged. This one needs a much less expensive foundation and no $240 crane. Even though we are carrying ninety-pound bags of cement up the hill ourselves, we consistently feel consolation about this project.

SHARING THE EXAMEN WITH OTHERS

One aspect of the examen that we especially appreciate is sharing it with each other. We find this one of the best ways we know to develop intimacy in families and communities. Sharing the examen allows us to enter the world of another in a simple and regular way. It also helps us grow in understanding and acceptance of how others differ from us. In our case, we sometimes discover that one person's consolation is another person's desolation.

For example, I (Matt) spend several weeks each summer writing with Dennis and Sheila in their home. One of the things I enjoy most is the $2.00 All-You-Can-Eat buffet on Friday nights at a local restaurant. It used to be $1.00, until this summer when they doubled the price on me. The plates are as tiny as saucers but you can go back as often as you want and fill up on ham, pizza, ribs, egg rolls, etc. There's always a large and noisy crowd of people, most of them drinking enough beer to more than pay for my four return trips through the line.

The first time all three of us went, we came home and did the examen afterwards. I shared that my consolation was the buffet and getting all I wanted of my favorite foods for $2.00. To my surprise, Sheila shared that her desolation was the buffet. Sheila makes everything by hand from all natural ingredients—she even grinds her own flour. She likes to serve lovely, quiet meals with candlelight and flowers. Now on Friday nights, Sheila blesses Dennis and me on our way to stuff ourselves at the buffet, and she has quiet time to work in her garden.

CHILDREN CAN DO THE EXAMEN

In our book, *Sleeping with Bread,* we wrote about the examen at much greater length than we can do here. Since then, many people have shared with us their experience of this process. Some have already been doing it in their own way for many years, and our book has simply affirmed or slightly refined their practice. Others have begun the examen for the first time. The stories that move us most are always those involving children, who can do the examen when they are as young as two years old. With children, the questions can be adapted to something like, "What was your happiest time today? What was your saddest time?" In a culture where children are constantly bombarded with advertisements and other messages about what they *should* want, the examen can help them stay in touch with the voice of God within themselves and know what they really *do* want.

One religious education teacher told us that she uses the examen with seven-year-olds preparing for the Sacrament of Reconciliation. She asks the children to reflect each day on when they felt close to themselves, others and God, and when they felt far away from themselves, others and God. Those moments of feeling far away help the children understand that "sin" is alienation, and it is these moments that they share in the Sacrament.

THE EXAMEN CAN HELP US WITH ANY PROBLEM

Like these children learning to identify alienation in their lives, you can do the examen over any issue or problem. For example, if you are struggling with depression, at the end of each day you can ask yourself, "What today helped me most with my depression? What helped me least?" If you are unsure of your vocation, you can ask yourself, "What way of using my gifts today helped me give and receive the most love? What way made it harder to give and receive love?"

As you conclude this book, you may be wondering which of these eight prayer processes to incorporate into your life and how to do it. You can ask yourself, "What in this book gave me the most life? What gave me the least life?" Because we can assume that God always wants to give us more life, the simple examen questions can guide us to greater wholeness in any situation.

❦ *Examen Process*

1. Create a quiet, prayerful space around you. You may wish to light a candle, as a symbol of how the light of God's presence shines through your everyday experience. Close your eyes and breathe deeply, breathing in the love of God that surrounds you.

2. Reflect back over your day, asking yourself for what moment you are most grateful and for what moment you are least grateful. You may wish to vary the questions in whatever way helps you to identify your consolation and desolation from the day. For example:

> When today did I give and receive the most love?
> When today did I give and receive the least love?

What moment today gave me the most life?
What moment today drained life out of me?

When today did I have the most sense of belonging to myself, others,
    God and the universe?
When today did I have the least sense of belonging?

3. Breathe in again the life you received in your moment of consolation and breathe God's love into your moment of desolation.

4. Give thanks for both moments and for what they have to teach you about what gives you life and what does not.

5. If you wish, share your moments with another person.

Epilogue

A Blue Cross of Iowa study found that prayer and meditation make people younger. In fact, for every year that a person meditates, that person will reverse his or her physiological age by one year. For example, if you start meditating at age forty-five, by the time you are age fifty-five your body's physiological age will be that of a thirty-five-year-old. Could this be why the longest living group of

people in the United States are nuns? We have proof positive, since the only nuns who have died are those who have stopped praying our prayers. We are planning a research project to see if those who do our prayers every day will ever die. If you never die, please contact us. Meanwhile, now that you have finished this book, look at yourself in the mirror and see the difference. Why not pray again and see if the rest of your wrinkles disappear?

Process for Group Sharing

Following is a suggested format for using this book as a course in healing prayer with a wide variety of groups. Such groups can be as diverse as the communities we have met during our retreats all over the world. These include 12-Step recovery groups, prison inmates, parish study groups, youth groups, patients in group psychotherapy, etc. The course can have eight sessions or it can be shortened to suit the needs of the group. This book may be accompanied by our tape series *Simple Ways to Pray for Healing,* or it may be used alone. Each member of the group will need a copy of this book. If you are using the audio or video tapes, you will need one set for the entire group.

This format takes 1½ to 2 hours for each session. Feel free to vary the format as needed. Normally groups meet once per week, but you may wish to vary the frequency of meetings. For example, you may wish to meet every two weeks or you may wish to have several sessions over one weekend.

I. Group Meetings

    A. Common Opening Prayer *(5 minutes)*

    B. Video or Audio Tape *(30 minutes)*
       If you do not have the tapes, simply review this week's chapter in the book and pray the prayer at the end of the chapter.

C. Silent Reflection *(3 minutes)*
    Quiet time to get in touch with what part of today's presentation moved your heart most deeply.

D. Guided Journaling *(Optional—10 minutes)*
    1. Write down what is in your heart. Write as if you were writing a letter to your best friend—Jesus or God as you understand God—sharing what you feel most deeply. Don't worry about having the "right" words, but only try to share your heart. If you find it more helpful, draw a picture rather than write a letter.
    2. Now get in touch with how God is responding to you, as He/She speaks to you from within. You might do this by asking what is the most loving response that Jesus or God as you understand God could possibly make to you in response to what you have just shared.
    3. Write God's response. Perhaps it will be just one word or one sentence. Or, perhaps it will be a simple drawing. You can be sure anything you write or draw that helps you to know more that you are loved is not just your own thoughts or imagination. It is at least part of what God wants to say to you.

E. Companion Sharing *(5 minutes minimum for each person to share his or her reaction to today's presentation and to the home experiences during the past week).* By the second session, each person should choose one or two companions for companion sharing and companion prayer. If possible, companions should remain together throughout the course.
    1. Share with your companion as much as you wish of what is in your heart from this week's presentation. Perhaps you will want to share what you have just written or drawn during the guided journaling.
    2. Share with your companion your experience at home since you last met, especially your prayer and journaling.
    3. Share with your companion what you are most grateful for now and how you need help from God.

F. Companion Prayer *(5–10 minutes of prayer for each person)*
    Pray for your companion as Jesus or God as you understand God would pray. Perhaps use the prayer process for praying with another on pages

65–66, or pray in any other way you wish. Give thanks for whatever your companion is most grateful for and pray for whatever healing your companion most wants. Then reverse roles and let your companion pray for you.

G. Group Sharing *(Optional—15 minutes minimum)*
Share with the whole group your response to this week's presentation and your experience at home since you last met. Some people may wish to share from their journals.

H. Closing Snack and Celebration
An open-ended time to enjoy one another and to continue sharing.

II. Preparation at Home Between Group Meetings

A. Daily Healing Prayer *(10 minutes or as long as you wish)*
Each day, pray the prayer at the end of that week's chapter in *Simple Ways to Pray for Healing.* For example, each day of the first week pray the prayer at the end of Chapter 1; each day of the second week pray the prayer at the end of Chapter 2; etc.

B. Daily Journal *(10 minutes)*
1. In writing or through a drawing, share with Jesus or with God as you understand God when during this prayer or during the day your heart was deeply moved.
2. Write or draw in your journal how Jesus or God responds to what you have shared. One way to get in touch with God's response is to write or draw the most loving response you can imagine.

Notes

Page 2

Larry Dossey, *Healing Words: The Power of Prayer and the Practice of Medicine* (New York: HarperCollins, 1992). Quote is from pages xviii and 205. On pages 251–253, Dr. Dossey summarizes some of the research on the effects of prayer and other spiritual practices on health. For example, a survey of twelve years of publication of the *American Journal of Psychiatry* and *Archives of General Psychiatry* found that 92 percent of the studies of prayer and spirituality showed benefit for mental health, 4 percent were neutral and 4 percent showed harm. A survey of ten years of publication of the *Journal of Family Practice* found that 83 percent of the studies showed benefit for physical health, 17 percent were neutral and none showed harm. See also Larry Dossey, *Prayer Is Good Medicine* (San Francisco: Harper, 1996), p. 66.

Charles Marwick, "Should Physicians Prescribe Prayer for Health?: Spiritual Aspects of Well-Being Considered," *JAMA*, Vol. 273, No. 20 (May 24/31, 1995), pp. 1561–1562. The author concludes by quoting David B. Larson, M.D., president of the National Institute for Healthcare Research:

> Spirituality and religion have important health benefits and more detailed studies using more accurate measures of this are warranted. . . . The question today is not whether there are health benefits, it is how these benefits can be obtained. We can no longer afford to neglect this important clinical variable.

Claudia Wallis, "Faith & Healing: Can Spirituality Promote Health?" *Time* (June 24, 1996), pp. 58–64.

The idea that the unused 90–95% of our neocortex is intended for higher consciousness and spirituality comes from Joseph Chilton Pearce, in his interview by Michael Toms, "Adventures of the Mind" (San Francisco: New Dimensions, 1996).

Page 3

Quote regarding the efficacy of prayer and religious affiliation is from a letter from Dr. Larry Dossey to Dr. Martin Parmentier, December 3, 1994. Used with Dr. Dossey's permission.

Page 8

Six-year study of 2428 men comparing death rates of pessimists and optimists was done by Dr. Susan Eberson at the Human Population Laboratory in Berkeley, California. Reported in *USA Today* (March 23, 1995).

Rabbi Harold Schulweis' work is described in Charles A. Cerami, "Half a Million Schindlers," *America* (October 15, 1994), pp. 13–17.

Pages 9–11

Bill W.'s story is found in *'Pass It On'* (New York: Alcoholics Anonymous World Services, 1979). Quotes about his first drink and his conversion experience are from pages 56 and 121. Quote about belonging and prayer is from *Twelve Steps and Twelve Reflections* (New York: Alcoholics Anonymous World Services, 1953), p. 105.

Page 11

On breathing as a way of connecting with all creation, see Brad Lernley, "Bio-dance," *The Washington Post Magazine* (February 23, 1986), p. 10. Cited in Louis M. Savary & Patricia Berne, *Kything: The Art of Spiritual Presence* (Mahwah, NJ: Paulist Press, 1988), p. 56.

Page 14

Conrad Baars, *Born Only Once* (Chicago: Franciscan Herald Press, 1975).

Pages 14–15

For a discussion of the Heisenberg Principle, see "Theology and the Heisenberg Uncertainty Principle" in Christopher Mooney, S.J., *Theology and Scientific Knowledge* (Notre Dame: University of Notre Dame Press, 1996).

For subatomic reality as either waves or particles, see Nick Herbert, "How Large Is Starlight?: A Brief Look at Quantum Reality," *Revision,* Vol. 10, No. 1 (Summer, 1987), pp. 31–35. See also Michael Talbot, *The Holographic Universe* (New York: HarperCollins, 1991), pp. 33–34.

Pages 15–17

Research on the doula is summarized in Marshall H. Klaus, John H. Kennell, and Phyllis H. Klaus, *Mothering the Mother: How a Doula Can Help You Have a Shorter, Easier, Healthier Birth* (Reading, MA: Addison-Wesley, 1993).

Page 17

For a discussion of memory as tuning in to a field, see Rupert Sheldrake, *The Presence of the Past* (New York: Times Books/Random House, 1988) and Michael Toms' interview with Rupert Sheldrake, "The Past Is Present" (San Francisco: New Dimensions, 1994). For Howard Gardner's Theory of Multiple Intelligences and the importance of love in learning, see Joseph Chilton Pearce, *Evolution's End* (San Francisco: Harper, 1992).

Page 19

Harville Hendrix' "flooding" exercise is demonstrated in Part 2 of his talk "Marriage as a Path to Wholeness" (Boulder, CO: Sounds True, 1993).

Research by Dr. John Gottman at the University of Washington was reported in his address, "What Predicts Divorce?" at the Erickson Foundation Conference on "Integrating Sexuality & Intimacy: The Challenge of Treating Couples in the '90s," Phoenix, AZ, May 17–19, 1996, and in *Psychology Today* (April, 1994), pp. 38–42.

Raymond L. Aaron, "The Annual Letters," in Jack Canfield and Mark Hansen, *A Second Helping of Chicken Soup for the Soul* (Deerfield Beach, FL: Health Communications, 1995), pp. 114–116.

Page 20

Rainer Maria Rilke. Source could not be located.

Page 22

The source for this quote, now widely attributed to Nelson Mandela, is Marianne Williamson, *A Return to Love* (San Francisco: Harper, 1992), pp. 188–189.

Page 26

For "hell" as originating in "gehenna" or "Gehinnom," see "Gehinnom" in *The Universal Jewish Encyclopedia,* Vol. 4 (New York: Ktav, 1969), pp. 520–521 and J.L. McKenzie, *Dictionary of the Bible* (Milwaukee: Bruce, 1965), pp. 300 and 801.

Pages 27–28

For Jesus' descent into hell see *The New Jerusalem Bible* (Garden City: Doubleday, 1985), footnote h for 1 Peter 3:19.

Quotes from Hans Urs von Balthasar are found in Medard Kehl and Werner Loser (eds.), *The Von Balthasar Reader* (New York: Crossroad, 1982), pp. 153 and 422. See also Hans Urs von Balthasar, *Dare We Hope? "That All Men Be Saved?"* (San Francisco: Ignatius Press, 1988), Chapter 7, "The Obligation to Hope for All," pp. 211–221. Balthasar is a prominent theologian known for his conservatism. Some say he is the favorite theologian of the present pope, John Paul II. John Sachs, S.J., summarizes Balthasar's position as follows:

> After examining the Scripture and the Church's liturgical, doctrinal and theological tradition, Balthasar concludes that while we may not claim to know the final outcome of human decision and divine judgment with certainty, we may hope that all will be saved. Indeed, it is our duty to do so. Only thus can the disciple truly express the loving solidarity of Christ, who died for all. . . . [Balthasar's] is a pointed, but not extreme position, quite consonant with Church teaching and the thought of most other major Catholic theologians. (In John R. Sachs, S.J., "Current Eschatology: Universal Salvation and the Problem of Hell," *Theological Studies,* 52 [1991], p. 232.)

Pages 28–29

Dr. Robert Stuckey, "You Gotta Have Hope," *New Catholic World,* Vol. 232, No. 1390 (July/August, 1989), pp. 160–161.

Page 29

Karl Rahner's statement about "unshakable hope" that all will be saved is found in *Foundations of Christian Faith* (New York: Seabury, 1978), p. 435. Cited in John R. Sachs, S.J., *op. cit.*, p. 242. Rev. Sachs' article is a survey of contemporary Roman Catholic theological opinion regarding the problem of hell. Our own position, like Balthasar's, is consistent with the principles which Sachs (as quoted above) found to be held by the majority of contemporary theologians.

Page 33

The five stages of dying were originally described by Elisabeth Kübler–Ross in her book *On Death and Dying* (New York: Macmillan, 1969).

Pages 33–35

Our application of the fives stages of dying to the process of healing any hurt first appeared in Dennis Linn and Matthew Linn, *Healing Life's Hurts: Healing Memories through the Five Stages of Forgiveness* (Mahwah, NJ: Paulist Press, 1978; Revised Edition 1993).

Page 42

Study of increased rate of heart attacks after a loved one's death reported by Murray Mittleman of Harvard Medical School in *Harvard Health Letter* (June, 1996), p. 8. Increased rate of depression reported in *Psychology Today* (November, 1995), p. 9.

Page 44

Maurice Zundel, *The Splendor of the Liturgy* (London: Sheed & Ward).

Page 45

Summary of Princeton research is from Larry Dossey, *Healing Words, op. cit.*, p. 49.

The relationship of love, empathy and compassion to the mind's ability to transcend space and time is discussed in Dossey, *Healing Words, op. cit.*, pp. 110–111. He quotes researcher F.W.H. Myers: "Love is a kind of exalted but unspecialized telepathy; the simplest and most universal expression of that mutual gravitation or kinship of spirits which is the foundation of the telepathic law."

Page 46

For "flashforwards" as part of near-death experiences, see Kenneth Ring, *Heading Toward Omega* (New York: William Morrow, 1985), pp. 186–187, cited in Michael Talbot, *The Holographic Universe* (New York: Harper Collins, 1991), pp. 253 and 270. For other characteristics of near-death experiences and for their after-effects, including increased ability to anticipate future events or to sense events in the present that are occurring at a distance, see Melvin Morse, *Transformed by the Light* (New York: Ballantine, 1992).

Page 51

Bell's theorem is summarized in Dossey, *Healing Words, op. cit.*, pp. 155–156 and Dossey, *Prayer Is Good Medicine, op. cit.*, pp. 31–32.

Page 53

A summary of Randolph Byrd's experiment and quote from William Nolan are found in Dossey, *Healing Words, op. cit.*, p. 180. See also Randolph C. Byrd and John Sherrill, "The Therapeutic Effects of Intercessory Prayer," *Journal of Christian Nursing,* Vol. 12, No. 1 (Winter, 1995), pp. 21–23.

Page 56

Dr. Braud's research was done at the Mind Research Foundation in San Antonio, Texas. Reported by Dr. Larry Dossey in a talk entitled "Science, Spirit & Soul" (Boulder, CO: Sounds True Recordings, 1991).

Page 63

A study by biologist Bernard Grad of McGill University in Montreal has demonstrated the efficacy of prayer when people who are sick themselves pray for other sick people. Cited in Bernie Siegel, *Peace, Love & Healing* (New York: Harper, 1989), p. 253. Dr. Karl Menninger understood this when he said, "Love cures two people, the person who gives it and the person who receives it." Cited in Bernie Siegel, *How to Live Between Office Visits* (New York: Harper, 1993), p. 173.

Quote regarding the ability of love to raise the immune system is from Bernie Siegel, *Love, Medicine & Miracles* (New York: Harper, 1986), p. 181.

An example of how plants respond to love is found in Larry Dossey, *Prayer Is Good Medicine, op. cit.*, pp. 166–173. Dr. Dossey tells the story of Rev. Karl Goodfellow, a Methodist minister in Iowa who discovered that praying for corn seeds and blessing cornfields resulted in better crops. Concerned about the number of farm failures in Iowa, Rev. Goodfellow then organized prayer partners for every one of the 12,000 farm families in his church district. They prayed not only for bountiful harvests but also for protection from accidents. The results have been not only better crops and fewer accidents, but an increase in compassion and care among everyone involved in the project. Rev. Goodfellow is now working with the University of Iowa to evaluate the results, and he plans to expand the project to include all the farms in the Midwest.

Page 75

Study of meditation and aging is found in Deepak Chopra, *Quantum Healing* (New York: Bantam, 1990), p. 194.

Resources for Further Growth
by the Authors

Books

Healing of Memories (1974). A simple guide to inviting Jesus into our painful memories to help us forgive ourselves and others.

Belonging: Bonds of Healing & Recovery (1993). Twelve Step recovery from any compulsive pattern is integrated with contemporary spirituality and psychology. This book helps the reader discover the genius underneath every addiction. Defines addiction as rooted in abuse and as our best attempt to belong to ourselves, others, God and the universe. Recovery comes from finding a better way to belong. May be used as follow-up to Chapters 1 and 2.

Good Goats: Healing Our Image of God (1994). We become like the God we adore. Thus, one of the easiest ways to heal ourselves and our society is to heal our image of God, so that we know a God who loves us at least as much as those who love us the most. Discusses whether God throws us into hell or otherwise vengefully punishes us, and the role of free will. Includes a question and answer section that gives the theological and scriptural foundation for the main text. We recommend this book as the most complete follow-up to Chapter 3.

Healing Spiritual Abuse & Religious Addiction (1994). Why does religion help some people grow in wholeness, yet seems to make others become more rigid and stuck? Discusses religious addiction and spiritual abuse, and offers ways of healing the shame-based roots of these behaviors. Includes how spiritual abuse can also be sexually abusive, and how scripture has often been used to reinforce religious addiction and spiritual abuse. Concludes with an image of healthy religion, in which we are free to do what Jesus would do. May be used as follow-up to Chapter 3.

Healing the Eight Stages of Life (1988). Based on Erik Erikson's developmental system, this book helps to heal hurts and develop gifts at each stage of life, from conception through old age. Includes healing ways our image of God has been formed and deformed at each stage. May be used as follow-up to Chapters 3 and 4.

Healing Life's Hurts: Healing Memories through the Five Stages of Forgiveness (1978, revised 1993). Contains a thorough discussion of the five stages of dying and how they apply to the process of forgiveness. This is our most complete resource on forgiveness and we recommend it as follow-up to Chapter 4.

Don't Forgive Too Soon: Extending the Two Hands That Heal (1997). When we are hurt, we are tempted to either act as a passive doormat or to strike back and escalate the cycle of violence. We can avoid both of these temptations and find creative responses to hurts by moving through the five stages of forgiveness. In so doing, we discover the two hands of nonviolence: one hand that stops the person who hurt us and the other that reaches out, calms that person and offers new life. This book has healing processes so simple that children can use them. May be used as follow-up to Chapters 4 and 6.

Healing the Greatest Hurt (1985). Healing the deepest hurt most people experience, the loss of a loved one, by learning to give and receive love with the deceased through the Communion of Saints. May be used as follow-up to Chapter 5.

Praying with Another for Healing (1984). Guide to praying with another to heal hurts such as sexual abuse, depression, loss of a loved one, etc. May be used as follow-up to Chapter 7.

To Heal as Jesus Healed (with Barbara Shlemon Ryan, 1978, revised 1997). This book, also on praying with another, emphasizes physical healing, including the healing power of the Sacrament of the Sick. May be used as follow-up to Chapter 7.

Sleeping with Bread: Holding What Gives You Life (1995). A simple process—for individuals and for families and others to share—of reflecting on each day's consolation and desolation. This process can help us get in touch each day with both hurts and healing, guide our decisions and help us find the purpose of our life. It offers a more thorough discussion of the examen presented in Chapter 8, including a question and answer section at the end.

These and other books by the authors (except *To Heal As Jesus Healed*) are available from Paulist Press, 997 Macarthur Blvd., Mahwah, NJ 07430, phone orders (800) 218-1903, FAX orders (800) 836-3161. *To Heal As Jesus Healed* is available from Resurrection Press, 77 West End Rd., Totowa, NJ, 07512, phone (877) 228-2410, FAX (973) 890-2410.

TAPES & COURSES
(for use alone, with a companion, or with a group)

Simple Ways to Pray for Healing (1998). Audio or videotapes to accompany this book.

Good Goats: Healing Our Image of God (1994). DVD or two-part videotape to accompany book (see above).

Healing Spiritual Abuse & Religious Addiction (1994). Audio tapes to accompany book (see above).

Belonging: Healing & 12 Step Recovery (1992). Audio or videotapes and a course guide to accompany book (see above), for use as a program of recovery.

Healing the Eight Stages of Life (1991). Tapes and a course guide that can be used with book (see above) as a course in healing the life cycle. Available in video and audio versions.

Prayer Course for Healing Life's Hurts (1983). Ways to pray for personal healing that integrate physical, emotional, spiritual and social dimensions. Book includes course guide, and tapes are available in video and audio versions.

Praying with Another for Healing (1984). Tapes that can be used with book (see above). Book includes course guide, and tapes are available in video and audio versions. *Healing the Greatest Hurt* (see above) may be used as supplementary reading for the last five of these sessions, which focus on healing of grief for the loss of a loved one.

Dying to Live: Healing through Jesus' Seven Last Words (with Bill & Jean Carr, 1983). How the seven last words of Jesus empower us to fully live the rest of our life. Tapes (available in video or audio versions) may be used with the book *Healing the Dying* (with Mary Jane Linn, 1979).

Audio tapes for all of these courses are available from Christian Video Library, 3914-A Michigan Ave., St. Louis, MO 63118, phone (314) 865-0729, FAX (314) 664-6128. For more information go to www.linnministries.org.

VIDEOTAPES ON A DONATION BASIS

To borrow any of the above videotapes, contact Christian Video Library (address and telephone above).

SPANISH BOOKS & TAPES

Several of the above books and tapes are available in Spanish. For information, contact Christian Video Library.

RETREATS & CONFERENCES

For retreats and conferences by the authors on the material in this book and on other topics in the resources listed above, contact Dennis, Sheila & Matthew Linn, c/o Re-Member Ministries, 3914-A Michigan Ave., St. Louis, MO 63118, phone (970) 476-9235 or (314) 865-0729, FAX (970) 476-9235 or (314) 664-6128, e-mail info@linnministries.com.

ABOUT THE AUTHORS

Dennis, Sheila and Matt Linn work together as a team, integrating physical, emotional and spiritual wholeness, having worked as hospital chaplains and therapists, and currently in leading retreats and spiritual companioning. They have taught courses on processes for healing in over forty countries and in many universities and hospitals, including a course to doctors accredited by the American Medical Association. Dennis and Matt are the co-authors of fifteen books, the last ten co-authored with Sheila. Their books include *Healing of Memories, Healing Life's Hurts* (revised 1993), *Healing the Dying* (with Sr. Mary Jane Linn), *To Heal as Jesus Healed* (with Barbara Shlemon Ryan, revised 1997), *Prayer Course for Healing Life's Hurts, Praying with Another for Healing, Healing the Greatest Hurt, Healing the Eight Stages of Life, Belonging: Bonds of Healing & Recovery, Good Goats: Healing Our Image of God, Healing Spiritual Abuse & Religious Addiction, Sleeping with Bread: Holding What Gives You Life,* and *Don't Forgive Too Soon: Extending the Two Hands That Heal.* These books have sold over a million copies in English and have been translated into more than fifteen different languages. Dennis and Sheila live in Colorado with their son John. Matt lives in a Jesuit community in Minneapolis.

ABOUT THE ILLUSTRATOR

Francisco Miranda lives in Mexico City. In addition to illustrating *Good Goats: Healing Our Image of God, Healing Spiritual Abuse & Religious Addiction, Sleeping with Bread: Holding What Gives You Life,* and *Don't Forgive Too Soon: Extending the Two Hands That Heal,* he has also written and illustrated several children's books.

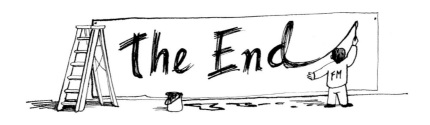